On the Evolution of Data Science and Machine Learning
ISBN: 9798304580908
Copyright © 2025 by Ibraheem Azeem

Table of Contents

Preface

Over the course of my career, I have had the privilege of working across various industries as both an engineer and a data scientist. My work has taken me from automating complex tasks to developing intelligent systems capable of predicting, adapting, and evolving. Through these experiences, I have come to a crucial realization: while data science and machine learning are becoming increasingly significant in shaping the future, many people still struggle to grasp the essence of these fields, their evolution, and their potential to transform the world. The challenge of explaining my work to friends, colleagues, and even professionals within the industry has fueled my desire to bridge this knowledge gap. Many are curious about why data science and machine learning have become so pivotal in today's world, how they have developed over time, and where they are heading in the future. This book is an attempt to answer those questions. My aim is to present the progression of data science and machine learning in a way that is accessible to everyone, regardless of their technical expertise. By educating readers on the history, current state, and future direction of these fields, I hope to inspire more people to engage with them, whether through professional pursuits or in everyday life.

I would like to extend special thanks to Ameta, the company where I had the opportunity to work on real-time AI projects. Ameta has developed a system that serves as a prime example of data science software, where raw data is processed and refined into meaningful insights for analysis. It is like a washing machine for data—where we input raw information, and it comes out refined and usable. I am proud to be the core developer of this application, and it has been instrumental in deepening my understanding of how data can be transformed into knowledge.

Understanding where data science comes from and where it is going can help us navigate the challenges and opportunities that lie ahead in this rapidly evolving, data-driven world. I invite you to join me on this journey of discovery into one of the most exciting and influential fields of our time.

1

Data Through Time

In Ancient Times, individuals recognized the value of gathering and evaluating data, even though their techniques were much more basic compared to modern methods. Despite lacking advanced technology, ancient civilizations were clever in utilizing simple tools and methods to collect information for purposes such as governance, trade, astronomy, and agriculture. Even in the past, data played a crucial role in decision-making and the structure of societies. The ancient Sumerians, one of the first civilizations, documented information as far back as 3100 BCE on clay tablets. They recorded information regarding trade, land ownership, and taxes. This was among the initial cases in which data was utilized to control economies and monitor resources. In the same way, the Babylonians were leaders in gathering astronomical information. Studying the stars and planets, they observed their movements to create calendars and forecast significant events such as eclipses. This was not simply out of curiosity; it assisted them in synchronizing their farming schedules with the seasonal changes.

On the Evolution of data Science and Machine Learning
Ibraheem Azeem

Ancient Egyptian farming along the Nile depended greatly on information. They monitored the annual floods closely to predict the ideal time for planting crops in the soil. This was not just guessing - they had thorough documentation that helped them understand the river's behavior and its impact on farming. Similarly, they conducted surveys to track the population for tax and allocation of resources. It was a method used to count the population of the kingdom and organize assignments for major projects like building the pyramids. In the Han Dynasty, the Chinese government conducted detailed population censuses to assist in tax collection and resource allocation. Comprehensive documentation of land ownership and crop yields was also kept to guarantee effective administration of agriculture, the primary pillar of the economy.

Astronomy played a significant role in ancient civilizations. The Greeks, for example, developed sophisticated methods for mapping the stars and planets. Ptolemy, a Greek astronomer, compiled a vast amount of astronomical data in his renowned work, *Almagest*. This contributed to a deeper understanding of the universe, aided in navigation, and helped organize timekeeping. Meanwhile, the Mayan civilization in the Americas used astronomical observations to create their intricate calendar system. They closely monitored celestial events, using the information to guide religious rituals, agricultural activities, and political decisions. In addition, data was vital for governance in ancient times. The Roman Empire, for instance, regularly conducted censuses to manage taxation, military recruitment, and social organization. These comprehensive efforts to assess the empire's population, geographical spread, and wealth distribution were crucial for maintaining the stability of both the Roman economy and its powerful military. Initial forms of data analysis were starting to develop in the field of mathematics. In ancient Greece, Eratosthenes used shadow measurements to make a precise estimation of the Earth's circumference. Ancient India played a significant role in advancing early mathematics and probability theory using actual data for important calculations in fields such as construction and astronomy.

Data gathering also had a notable impact on business and economic activities. Civilizations like the Phoenicians, renowned for their advanced trade networks, recorded data about traded items, paths, and costs. These documents helped traders predict market demands and plan their trips efficiently. The Silk Road connected Asia and Europe, serving as a vital trade route where merchants exchanged information on goods, markets, and prices, playing a key role in the development of the global economy in ancient times. Additionally, understanding celestial events and patterns was essential for religious practices. Ancient Egyptian priests observed celestial events to create a timeline for religious festivities. The exact character of these events was essential as religious ceremonies were closely connected to agriculture and changes in seasons. Landmarks like Stonehenge in England show evidence of data collection, as their alignment with the solstices suggests that the builders were tracking the sun's movement to identify significant seasonal dates. In Christian and Islamic societies, the collection and analysis of data were important, even

10

if not always recognized in the formal way we understand today. Both religious traditions played a role in shaping the development of data management, from overseeing governance and religious practices to advancing scientific investigation. During the middle ages, the Church played a key role in preserving knowledge and maintaining records in Christian culture. For instance, monasteries served as centers for education and academic research. Monks painstakingly transcribed texts, including religious scriptures and significant works of science, history, and philosophy. This was among the first methods of gathering information, where knowledge was saved for generations to come. An example illustrating this was the requirement for astronomical information to establish the date of Easter, a crucial element in the Christian calendar. This requirement eventually resulted in the creation of more advanced calendar systems, culminating in the establishment of the Gregorian calendar, which was formulated through years of studying celestial patterns.

During the Christian era, governments also heavily depended on data collection. The well-known Domesday Book of 1086, ordered by William the Conqueror, is a remarkable illustration of early governance based on data. The thorough examination of England's territory, population, and assets offered in-depth understanding for improved tax collection and land administration, demonstrating the organized collection of data to govern the realm effectively. At a more common level, the Church's responsibility in upholding parish documents, like recording births, deaths, and

On the Evolution of data Science and Machine Learning
Ibraheem Azeem

marriages, became crucial for providing information not just for religious reasons but also for civil governance.

During the Islamic Golden Age, data collection and utilization flourished greatly in fields like science, mathematics, and astronomy within Islamic culture. Islamic scholars were heavily involved in conducting empirical studies, collecting and examining data to enhance human knowledge of the world. In the field of astronomy, notable figures such as "Al-Battani" and Al-"Tusi" made significant contributions by collecting accurate data on the movements of celestial bodies. Their observations were crucial for religious purposes such as establishing prayer times and the Islamic calendar, which is based on lunar cycles rather than just for scientific interest. In the same way, Islamic mathematicians like Al-Khwarizmi, known for creating algebra, utilized information that laid the groundwork for modern mathematics and computer science.

Religion influenced the gathering of information in Islamic society using the "Isnad" system for Hadith studies. This system meticulously traced the succession of people who transmitted the teachings, ensuring the trustworthiness of religious texts. One of the earliest methods of validating data sources, this practice foreshadowed modern academic protocols such as citation and peer evaluation. Muslim leaders also collected data necessary to rule vast empires, such as detailed information on land ownership, taxes, and population statistics. This data was essential for maintaining economic stability and organizing military campaigns, especially in large empires like the Abbasid Caliphate and later the Ottoman Empire.

Different cultures created innovative methods for gathering and analyzing information, paving the way for progress in modern science, business, and finance. Even though their techniques may have been basic by today's standards, the fundamental concept of utilizing data for decision-making was firmly established. The advancements achieved by these societies, whether through resource management, forecasting celestial occurrences, or administering large territories, highlight the importance of gathering and interpreting data in human progress. Their advancements influenced their own communities and set the foundation for our current perception and utilization of data. The lasting impact still shapes contemporary data science, research, and decision-making across various fields, illustrating the profound roots of these practices in historical cultures.

1.1. From Manual Record-Keeping to Digital Data Infrastructure

During the early stages of society, manual tracking was the main way to record information. Ancient civilizations used objects like clay tablets, papyrus scrolls, and eventually paper records to record important details such as trade deals, taxes, and population numbers. Keeping track of these records manually demanded a considerable investment of time and effort for their storage, organization, and retrieval. While the techniques were straightforward, the influence of this information on governing systems, business practices, and decision-making was significant, enabling societies to maintain organization and efficiently track their assets.

The transition from manual to digital data systems started when computing technology emerged in the mid-1900s. The emergence of electronic computers signaled a shift, enabling quicker and more precise data processing and storage. The emergence of early databases like flat files and hierarchical models aimed to improve data management and organization efficiency. As technology advanced, industries started moving from traditional paper records to digital databases, decreasing mistakes and simplifying management of vast amounts of information. This shift drastically altered the way businesses, governments, and organizations functioned, setting the groundwork for the current era of data handling. Today, the complexity and capability of digital data infrastructure has increased dramatically. Due to the emergence of the internet, cloud computing, and big data technologies, data can be gathered, saved, and examined on larger scales than ever before. Large data centers, linked by fast networks, form

Figure 1: Cave Paintings to Cloud Computing: The Evolution of Data Storage (Blog)

14

the foundation of this worldwide digital infrastructure, allowing for instant data processing and understanding. Modern database systems like relational and NoSQL databases have taken the place of manual techniques, enabling the effective storage and retrieval of large datasets. The shift towards digital infrastructure has revolutionized various sectors, making data-driven decision-making standard in fields like healthcare and finance, while also raising new challenges related to privacy, security, and data management. To gain a deeper understanding of this progression, we will explore each phase in detail—beginning with the early era of manual documentation, then transitioning to the rise of digital technology, and finally examining the contemporary data systems that underpin today's information-centric society.

1.2. Manual Record-Keeping: The Early Days

The act of manually recording information played a crucial role in ancient civilizations, serving as the main method for documenting important details and handling daily activities. Past civilizations, like those in Mesopotamia, Egypt, and China, created different methods to record important information such as trade deals, farming output, taxes, and religious rituals. Clay tablets, stone inscriptions, and papyrus scrolls were frequently utilized for documenting this information. Nevertheless, these techniques, while innovative in their era, encountered substantial obstacles that hindered their overall

On the Evolution of data Science and Machine Learning
Ibraheem Azeem

effectiveness and dependability in the end. One of the major concerns regarding manual record keeping was the susceptibility of the materials to physical damage. Clay tablets might break or splinter, dampness or insects could damage papyrus scrolls, and stone inscriptions, although sturdier, could deteriorate due to weathering in the end. Consequently, the information meticulously documented by these communities may easily disappear or be harmed, posing challenges for future generations to retrieve crucial data. Conflicts and attacks worsened the situation even more. In times of conflict, valuable records were often lost due to the destruction of libraries, archives, and record-keeping centers. The loss of the Library of Alexandria, for instance, is a famous case where extensive knowledge was permanently destroyed because of conflict and flames. Another significant obstacle was the laborious process of keeping records manually.

Maintaining records required a group of skilled scribes trained in literacy. This process was often slow, sometimes taking several days or even weeks to document large volumes of information. The lack of standardization in record-keeping systems compounded the issue, as different civilizations or regions used various formats, symbols, and languages to record data. This inconsistency made it difficult to organize and access records effectively, limiting their usefulness for large-scale administrative tasks and hindering the sharing of information.

Furthermore, the immense challenge of storing and categorizing large quantities of physical records presented a persistent issue. As time passes, archives may become packed with records decaying from

Figure 2. Image taken from Cave Paintings to the Cloud: The History of Data Storage

inadequate storage or lost without proper organization systems. This lack of efficiency led to the possibility of older records being misplaced or overlooked, causing interruptions in the consistency of governance and economic planning. In numerous instances, the inability to uphold and effectively handle records led to the downfall of certain societies, as they faced challenges in keeping precise records of resources, population, and trade.

17

Despite these limitations, manual record keeping laid the foundation for the sophisticated data management systems we use today. It helped ancient societies advance their economies, track populations, and manage resources, even though it was a slow, labor-intensive, and vulnerable process.

1.3.   The Emergence of Early Digital Systems

The shift from manual documentation to early digital systems was a crucial moment in the development of data management. Throughout the 20th century, the demand for enhanced techniques to manage large volumes of data grew as businesses, governments, and scientific institutions developed and expanded. The emergence of electronic computers in the mid-20th century started to meet these requirements by offering a groundbreaking capacity to automate computations and handle information. The creation of early computers like the ENIAC in the 1940s paved the way for this change.

According to Paul E. Ceruzzi's *A History of Modern Computing* (MIT Press, 2003), although primitive by today's standards, these early systems were revolutionary in their ability to process large amounts of data quickly. In the early days of digital systems, computers were primarily used for scientific calculations, particularly in military and

Figure 3: Early Computer build by German Engineer Konrad Zasu

research institutions. During World War II, technology such as the Colossus computer was created to crack German encryption, while the ENIAC was utilized for military calculations.

According to Martin Campbell-Kelly's book *Computer: A History of the Information Machine*, the early systems used vacuum tubes and punch cards for input, storage, and processing. Despite being bulky and complex, these early computers were far more efficient than manual methods. During this period, the first programmable computers were developed, capable of being reconfigured for different tasks—a key advancement that paved the way for more versatile digital systems. In the 1950s and 1960s, the commercial computer industry began to grow, driven by companies such as IBM, UNIVAC, and NCR. The introduction of the IBM 650 and UNIVAC I, primarily designed for business applications, revolutionized data processing in sectors like finance, insurance, and government administration. Businesses are relying more on digital systems for tasks like payroll processing, inventory management, and accounting, as stated by James W. Cortada in *Before the Computer (Princeton University*

19

Press, 1993). Early machines were initially operated with punch cards and demanded skilled specialists, but they initiated the widespread digitization in the business sector.

As technology advanced, data storage methods also evolved. Early computers relied on magnetic drums and punched tapes, which were inefficient for storing large amounts of data. However, the introduction of magnetic core memory and the development of hard disk drives in the late 1950s revolutionized data storage. IBM's release of the 305 RAMAC, the first computer to include a hard disk drive, allowed businesses to efficiently store much larger volumes of data in a compact space. In his book *The Innovators: How a Group of Hackers, Geniuses, and Geeks Created the Digital Revolution* (Simon & Schuster, 2014), Walter Isaacson discusses how these innovations paved the way for the advanced digital storage systems we rely on today, enabling faster data access and improved processing capabilities.

By the late 1960s and early 1970s, modern digital systems were firmly established. The rise of integrated circuits and the shift from bulky vacuum-tube technology to smaller, more efficient transistors enhanced the capabilities and accessibility of computers. As businesses began adopting these systems, databases became essential tools for storing and retrieving large amounts of structured data. The introduction of the relational database model by Edgar F. Codd in 1970, as highlighted in C.J. Date's *An Introduction to Database Systems* (Addison-Wesley, 2003), marked a significant

On the Evolution of data Science and Machine Learning
Ibraheem Azeem

advancement in data management, offering greater flexibility and efficiency. This period laid the groundwork for the rapid expansion of digital technology in the subsequent decades, solidifying the fundamental principles of modern computing and data storage.

1.4. The Growth of Digital Data Infrastructure

As technology advanced, the ability to store, process, and analyze data also improved. In the 1990s, there was a quick growth in digital data infrastructure, thanks to improvements in computing power, networking, and data storage. The internet's advancement was essential in this change, allowing for the global sharing, transfer, and real-time access of data.

Cloud computing, which emerged in the 2000s, continued to transform data infrastructure by offering scalable and affordable options for storing data and processing information. Companies no longer needed to have costly in-house servers; instead, they could remotely store and access their data, cutting costs and improving versatility. Major cloud platforms like **Amazon Web Services (AWS)**, **Microsoft Azure**, and **Google Cloud Platform (GCP)** provide diverse architectures and tools to support modern data storage and processing needs. These platforms offer solutions for object storage, databases, big data analytics, and even advanced features like machine learning integrations. For those curious about cloud computing, resources like provider documentation, online tutorials, or certification programs can be great starting points for further exploration.

21

Simultaneously, the implementation of enterprise resource planning (ERP) systems enabled businesses to combine different business operations like accounting, supply chain management, and human resources into a cohesive data framework. These systems enhanced the transmission of data between departments, leading to improved decision-making and operational efficiency. Major ERP systems like SAP and Oracle have been widely embraced by big companies globally, solidifying the importance of digital infrastructure in today's business operations.

Electronic health records (EHR) systems revolutionized patient care in healthcare by digitizing patient records, enabling healthcare providers in various locations to access them. This change increased the level of care, decreased medical mistakes, and made medical research easier by offering a large amount of information for examination. Likewise, digital data infrastructure in education facilitated the creation of student information systems (SIS) and learning management systems (LMS), improving administrative efficiency and promoting individualized student learning.

1.5. The Foundation of Data Science

In recent decades, data creation has surged due to rapid advancements in technology, driven largely by the expansion of the internet, social media, and the Internet of Things (IoT). This unprecedented flow of data gathered in real-time from countless sources has brought both opportunities and challenges. Organizations are rethinking how they store, process, and analyze this vast volume of information.

At the heart of this transformation is the evolution of data storage. Traditional data management systems had limited capacity, often relying on physical storage methods that restricted data accessibility and analytical potential. However, with the advent of cloud computing and distributed database technologies, companies now have scalable, flexible storage solutions. These technologies have made large-scale data storage and fast retrieval both possible and affordable, laying a foundation for advanced analysis.

The growth of big data analytics further accelerated digital infrastructure development. Businesses recognized that valuable insights could be gained by analyzing complex, massive datasets, and invested in tools capable of handling such data. Distributed processing frameworks like Hadoop and Apache Spark emerged, allowing rapid processing of large datasets and enabling decision-making based on data insights. This shift sparked the development of innovative analytical methods and techniques, pushing the boundaries of what data analysis could achieve.

Alongside these advancements, data analysis tools have become more user-friendly and accessible, reshaping how organizations engage with data. Intuitive software now allows professionals to perform complex analyses and create visualizations without deep technical expertise. This accessibility has broadened data use across industries, promoting a data-driven culture in various fields and

23

underscoring the need for a structured approach to data analysis practices.

These technological advances, the increasing complexity of data and the rising demand for data-based insights contributed to the emergence of data science as a unique discipline. Data science blends elements of statistics, computer science, and domain expertise, empowering organizations to unlock actionable insights, make informed decisions, and drive innovation. Today, data science is not just about handling data—it is about using it to understand and shape the world, marking a pivotal step forward in our ability to analyze and apply information effectively.

2

Data Science: Turning Data to Knowledge

The transformation of raw data into actionable insights has undergone significant evolution in recent decades. In the early days of computing, the sheer volume of data generated was often overwhelming, with storage and retrieval posing substantial challenges. However, as technology progressed, experts began to recognize the potential of data analysis to uncover valuable insights. This realization led to the emergence of data science as a distinct discipline. In *Data Science for Business*, Foster Provost and Tom Fawcett emphasize that the core purpose of data science is to extract insights from data to inform and enhance decision-making.

The 1960s and 1970s were a pivotal time for data analysis, with researchers creating advanced statistical methods and data systems. At this time, the introduction of databases enabled more effective storage and retrieval of data. Edgar F. Codd's research on relational databases transformed the way data was structured and retrieved, highlighting the significance of organizing data for efficient analysis. Codd's principles established the foundation for contemporary database management systems and emphasized the importance of accurate data for acquiring knowledge.

On the Evolution of data Science and Machine Learning
Ibraheem Azeem

As the volume of data grew rapidly, interest in data mining surged during the 1980s and 1990s. Data mining focused on uncovering patterns and relationships within large datasets. Scholars like Piatetsky-Shapiro and Roiger emphasized the importance of extracting valuable insights from data in their book *Data Mining: Concepts and Techniques*. This shift in focus, from merely storing data to analyzing it, marked a significant milestone in how organizations viewed data, as they began to recognize its value as a strategic asset.

The emergence of the internet in the late 1990s resulted in a significant increase in the volume of data, giving birth to the idea of "big data." This fresh approach necessitated creative strategies for analyzing data, leading researchers and professionals to delve into sophisticated statistical techniques and algorithms. The book *Big Data: A Revolution That Will Transform How We Live, Work, and Think* by Viktor Mayer-Schönberger and Kenneth Cukier shows how the growing amount and diversity of data required new analysis methods, changing how businesses made decisions and formulated strategies.

The formal recognition of data science as a separate discipline occurred in the early 2000s. Prominent individuals such as DJ Patil and Hilary Mason have started promoting the importance of merging domain knowledge with statistical analysis and computational skills. In article titled *Data Science: A Comprehensive Overview*, they expressed the concept that data science includes not just analyzing data but also interpreting and communicating insights obtained from that analysis. This cross-

On the Evolution of data Science and Machine Learning
Ibraheem Azeem

disciplinary strategy established data science as a key element in multiple fields such as business, healthcare, and social sciences.

With the development of the field, the significance of data visualization became more noticeable. Edward Tufte's book *The Visual Display of Quantitative Information* highlighted the importance of using visuals to help people understand and act on complex data. Data scientists found resonance in Tufte's principles of presenting data visually for improved understanding and decision-making by emphasizing clarity, precision, and efficiency. Moreover, the rise of open-source tools like R and Python has made data analysis techniques more accessible to the public. These tools allowed researchers and analysts with varied backgrounds to participate in data science, promoting a culture of teamwork and creativity. As stated by Hadley Wickham in *R for Data Science*, the availability of such tools enables people to use data for understanding, regardless of their education or academic experience.

Recently, data ethics has become a more prominent topic in conversations about data science. Both experts and professionals are now examining the process of gathering, utilizing, and analyzing data, acknowledging the risk of partiality and improper handling. Book *Weapons of Math Destruction* by Cathy O'Neil underscore the societal impacts of decision-making based on data and the importance of ethical guidelines in the field of data science.

Currently, data science sits at the crossroads of technology, statistics, and domain knowledge, highlighting a deep comprehension of transforming data into insights. The transition from unprocessed data to practical findings involves an ongoing advancement of tools, methods, and approaches. As emphasized in *Data Science for Dummies* by Anasse Bari, Mohamed Chaouchi, and Toby Meyer, the future of data science depends on its capacity to adjust and create in reaction to new challenges and opportunities in a constantly evolving environment.

The emergence of data science marks a new chapter in the quest for knowledge through data analysis. It does not just symbolize a subject of research, but a complete structure for comprehending and utilizing the potential of data in making decisions. The process of turning data into knowledge will keep evolving with new technology and methods, shaping industries and society in the future.

2.1. What is Data Science?

Data science involves using data to uncover valuable insights, combining both art and science. A domain integrates different fields like statistics, mathematics, computer science, and expertise in a specific area to understand unprocessed data and apply it in tackling practical issues. In today's world driven by data, data science is crucial for making decisions, fostering innovation, and comprehending intricate systems. According to IBM:

"Data science combines math and statistics, specialized programming, advanced analytics, artificial intelligence (AI) and machine learning with specific subject matter expertise to uncover actionable insights hidden in an organization's data. These insights can be used to guide decision making and strategic planning"

28

Data science is grounded in key principles that guide the ethical gathering and analysis of information. Closely connected to data science is data mining, which focuses on extracting valuable insights from data by applying specialized techniques based on these principles. Numerous algorithms and advanced methods are used in data mining, each bringing unique intricacies. These methods are widely applied across various functional areas in the business world.

In marketing, data science plays a key role in targeted marketing, online advertising, and recommendation systems, enabling businesses to understand and predict customer behavior. Customer relationship management (CRM) systems use data science to analyze customer actions, helping businesses reduce attrition and enhance customer value.

In the financial industry, data science is essential for assessing credit risk, making trading decisions, detecting fraud, and monitoring operations. Major retailers like Walmart and Amazon advantage data science across their operations, from marketing strategies to optimizing their supply chains. Many businesses today have distinguished themselves by effectively using data science, with some even evolving into data-mining-driven companies.

2.2. Evolution of Data Science

In recent years, data science has experienced substantial growth, shifting from a specialized area to a crucial aspect of decision-making in multiple industries. The shift is motivated by various factors, such

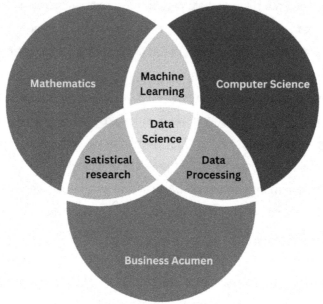

Figure 4: Data Science

as the rapid increase in data creation, improvements in computing capabilities, and the evolution of complex analytical methods. In the passage below, we examine the advancements of data science in recent years and its various uses in different industries, including the military.

2.2.1. Traditional Analytics to Big Data

On the Evolution of data Science and Machine Learning
Ibraheem Azeem

Historically, data analysis relied heavily on established statistical techniques and relatively small, structured data sets. Analysts applied methods such as descriptive statistics, hypothesis testing, and regression analysis to extract insights, often using spreadsheet programs and statistical software for basic calculations and analysis. However, as data volumes and complexity surged, the limitations of traditional analytics became increasingly evident. Organizations struggled to manage the growing influx of data generated from a wide range of sources, including customer transactions, social media interactions, and sensor data. This challenge prompted a shift in data analysis practices, marking the onset of a new era where conventional methods proved insufficient for an increasingly data-driven world. The rise of the internet and digital technologies has caused a significant increase in data creation, resulting in the emergence of big data. Currently, companies are overwhelmed by large quantities of data being produced constantly from customer engagements to IoT gadgets and social media use. This large amount of information brings difficulties and chances for businesses. In contrast with conventional datasets, big data is typically identified by its size, diversity, and speed, necessitating innovative approaches for storage, processing, and analysis. Hadoop and Apache Spark were developed to tackle these problems by offering scalable options for handling and examining big amounts of data. These frameworks empower organizations

31

to utilize big data effectively, unveiling previously concealed insights and enabling better decision-making through a thorough comprehension of their data environment.

The shift from traditional analytics to big data has driven the need for more sophisticated analytical frameworks that extend beyond basic statistical approaches. Today's data analysis involves a broad array of advanced techniques, including machine learning, data mining, and real-time analytics. These methods enable organizations to extract more comprehensive and actionable insights from their data, allowing them to identify patterns, predict future outcomes, and make more decisions that are informed. As a result, businesses are able to leverage data in ways that were previously unattainable with conventional analytics, providing them with a competitive edge in an increasingly data-driven landscape. By analyzing and processing unstructured data such as text, images, and videos, companies can uncover new opportunities to understand customer behavior and market trends. For instance, predictive analytics can forecast customer preferences based on past data, while sentiment analysis gauges public opinion through social media interactions. As businesses increasingly recognize the strategic value of their data, the advancement of analytics continues to reshape industries, driving innovation and fostering a data-driven decision-making culture.

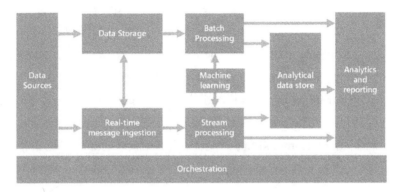

Figure 5: Shows the logical components that fit into a big data architecture. Individual solutions may not contain every item in this diagram. © Microsoft

2.2.2. Raise of Machine Learning

The emergence of machine learning and artificial intelligence (AI) has transformed the manner in which organizations handle and examine data. With the gathering of more vast and intricate datasets by businesses, traditional analytical techniques are frequently inadequate in revealing patterns and insights. Machine learning, enables systems to understand patterns, make predictions, and learn from data without needing specific instructions. This feature allows companies to streamline decision-making processes, elevate customer interactions, and boost operational effectiveness. Sectors such as healthcare, finance, and retail are using machine learning to create predictive models for various strategic purposes, including personalized marketing campaigns and fraud detection systems.

As we further explore the development of data science, it is crucial to acknowledge the significant impact that machine learning and AI have in this field. These technologies have changed data from just being numbers into valuable insights that can influence business strategies and societal trends. In the next chapter, we will delve deeper into its basic principles, techniques, and practical uses, demonstrating machine learning essential role in the field of data science and significant influence on diverse sectors.

2.2.3. Accessibility of Data Science Tools

The availability of data science tools has greatly made the field more accessible, allowing a wider variety of people and businesses to use data analytics effectively. Previously, data science was mainly restricted to specialized professionals with advanced degrees in statistics, computer science, or related fields. Non-experts can more easily visualize and analyze data now with the rise of user-friendly platforms like Tableau, Google Data Studio, and Microsoft Power BI. These tools frequently include user-friendly interfaces and ready-made templates that enable users to produce conclusions without needing advanced technical abilities. Consequently, diverse teams' perspectives can be utilized by organizations to make better decisions and promote a data-driven culture at different levels of the organization.

Furthermore, the increased popularity of open-source coding languages such as Python and R has also made data science more accessible. These programming languages provide a variety of libraries and frameworks like Pandas, NumPy, and scikit-learn that make complex data processing easier and allow users to create advanced models. The tools being open-source means that the community can constantly improve and contribute to them, making advanced data science techniques more accessible to those interested in data analysis. Platforms like Coursera, edX, and various YouTube channels offer easily accessible educational materials that enable individuals to enhance their skills at their own speed and apply them in practical situations.

The increasing availability of data science tools not only gives power to individuals but also has wider effects on innovation and economic development. Small companies and new businesses can now have a fairer chance to compete by using data-driven insights to drive their strategies and improve operations. Moreover, with the growing awareness of the importance of data analytics, there is a rising need for employees who are skilled in data interpretation, leading educational institutions to integrate data science into their course offerings. This change leads to a workforce that becomes more skilled in

Figure 6: Data Science Tools Official Icons

35

analyzing data, ultimately promoting a culture of making decisions based on data in different industries.

2.2.4. Focus on Ethics and Data Privacy

With the growth of data science, the importance of ethics and data privacy has become more crucial. Due to the widespread availability of big data and the capability to gather extensive information from different sources, ethical concerns regarding data usage have become increasingly important. Organizations are required to maneuver through intricate legal and ethical terrains, making sure they manage personal data with responsibility and transparency. Responsible data practices include securing permission from individuals before gathering their data, and putting in place strong data security measures to protect sensitive information. The GDPR in Europe displays how regulations are adapting to safeguard individuals' rights in a world that relies more on data.

Furthermore, the consequences of data misuse can have extensive effects, affecting both individuals and the credibility and reliability of organizations. Instances of data breaches and unauthorized data sharing have brought attention to the weaknesses present in data collection methods, resulting in public outcry and heightened oversight from regulators. Consequently, companies are more likely to focus on ethical data governance frameworks that involve routine audits, minimizing data, and holding individuals accountable. Organizations can enhance their credibility and build trust among consumers by incorporating ethical considerations into their data strategies, which also helps in reducing risks.

There is also a focus on ethical issues and data privacy when discussing the responsible utilization of artificial intelligence and machine learning. As algorithms become increasingly advanced, there is a growing recognition of the possible prejudices that may result from the data utilized in training these models. Dealing with these biases necessitates a dedication to ethical procedures in collecting data, preprocessing, and evaluating models. By prioritizing ethical practices in AI and data science, organizations can develop more just and inclusive systems that mirror the varied demographics of their target audiences.

2.3.   Emergence of Data Driven Cultures

The rise of data-Driven cultures in companies is a major change in how decisions and strategies are developed. As companies are starting to understand the importance of data, they are shifting from making decisions based on gut feelings to using data insights for a more evidence-based approach. This transformation necessitates a shift in culture, viewing data not just because of operations but also as a valuable asset guiding all business decisions. Leaders are essential in cultivating this culture through advocating for data literacy, promoting team collaboration, and showing dedication to data-driven decision-making.

In order to foster a culture that values data, companies need to dedicate resources and provide training so that all employees can effectively use and interpret data. This consists of providing data analysis workshops, giving access to data visualization tools, and promoting collaborations between departments to exchange insights and best practices. When employees are confident in handling data, they are more likely to help foster a culture that prioritizes making decisions based on evidence. Additionally, businesses have the ability to create key performance indicators (KPIs) that specifically align with results from data analysis, emphasizing the significance of data in accomplishing strategic goals.

The advantages of a culture based on data go further than just enhancing decision-making; they also promote innovation and adaptability in organizations. Through constant evaluation of data and addressing emerging trends, businesses can adjust to market shifts efficiently and discover potential avenues for expansion. For example, businesses that use customer data to improve their product offerings or enhance user experiences typically have a competitive edge in their markets. In today's competitive business environment, it is vital for organizations to prioritize developing a data-driven culture to ensure long-term success in harnessing the power of data.

2.4.   Different Techniques in Data Science

Data science encompasses a variety of models and techniques that enable the extraction of valuable insights from data. These techniques can be broadly categorized into statistical approaches, machine learning algorithms, data manipulation methods, and visualization tools. Below is a brief overview of key data science techniques and algorithms.

2.4.1. Statistical Models

Statistical models are important tools in data science for analyzing, interpreting, and making conclusions based on data. These models serve as mathematical representations of the relationships between variables and are essential for understanding patterns, trends, and dependencies in datasets. Statistical models provide a framework for making inferences about a population based on a subset of data. These models help in approximating associations, predicting outcomes, and assessing theories. There are typically two main types: descriptive and inferential.

- **Descriptive Models**

  Descriptive models include summarizing and describing dataset characteristics, providing information on measures of central tendency (mean, median, mode), variability (variance, standard deviation), and data distribution (normal distribution, skewness).

- **Inferential Models**

39

Inferential models allow researchers to make predictions about a bigger group of people by analyzing a smaller sample of data. They include hypothesis testing, confidence intervals, and regression analysis.

2.4.2. Types of Statistical Models

Linear Regression

Linear regression is a statistical method that involves adjusting a linear equation to fit observed data in order to model the relationship between a dependent variable and one or more independent variables, assuming a linear relationship between them. It is commonly used for making predictions and analyzing patterns, such as predicting sales using advertising expenses or estimating property values using factors such as size, location, and age. The linear regression model can be expressed as the equation:

$$Y = \beta_0 + \beta_1 X_1 + \ldots + \beta_n X_n + \epsilon$$

Where Y is the dependent variable, X stands for the independent variables, β represents the coefficients, and ε signifies the error term.

Code example:

```
import numpy as np

# Sample data (X as independent variable, Y as dependent variable)

X = np.array([1, 2, 3, 4, 5])

Y = np.array([2, 3, 5, 7, 11])

# Custom linear regression (calculating slope and intercept using the least
squares method)

def linear_regression(X, Y):

  n = len(X)

  X_mean = np.mean(X)

  Y_mean = np.mean(Y)

  # Calculate slope (b1) and intercept (b0)

  numerator = sum((X - X_mean) * (Y - Y_mean))

  denominator = sum((X - X_mean) ** 2)

  slope = numerator / denominator

  intercept = Y_mean - slope * X_mean

  return slope, intercept


# Calculate slope and intercept
```

On the Evolution of data Science and Machine Learning
Ibraheem Azeem

```
slope, intercept = linear_regression(X, Y)

# Predicted Y values

Y_pred = slope * X + intercept

print(f"Slope: {slope}")

print(f"Intercept: {intercept}")

print(f"Predicted Y: {Y_pred}")
```

In this implementation, the slope and intercept are calculated using the least squares formula. The linear_regression function derives these values from the input arrays X and Y. The predicted Y values are determined by using the equation $Y = mX+b$.

Logistic Regression

Logistic regression is utilized for categorical outcome variables, like binary outcomes such as success/failure or yes/no, to determine the probability of a given input being classified into a specific category. It is widely used in areas such as healthcare (for predicting disease occurrence), finance (for assessing credit risk), and marketing (for detecting customer turnover). The logistic regression model utilizes the logistic function to restrict the result to a range from zero to one, which can be understood as a probability. The formula is:

On the Evolution of data Science and Machine Learning
Ibraheem Azeem

$$P(Y = 1) = \frac{1}{1 + e^{-(\beta_0 + \beta_1 X_1 + \cdots + \beta_n X_n)}}$$

Code example:

```
def logistic_regression(X, Y, lr=0.01, epochs=1000):

  m = X.shape[0]

  weights = np.zeros(X.shape[1])

  bias = 0

  for _ in range(epochs):

    # Linear combination

    linear_model = np.dot(X, weights) + bias

    y_pred = sigmoid(linear_model)

    # Calculate gradients

    dw = (1 / m) * np.dot(X.T, (y_pred - Y))

    db = (1 / m) * np.sum(y_pred - Y)

    # Update weights and bias

    weights -= lr * dw

    bias -= lr * db

  return weights, bias

# Sample data
```

```
X = np.array([[1], [2], [3], [4], [5]])  # Independent variable

Y = np.array([0, 0, 1, 1, 1])  # Binary outcome

# Apply logistic regression

weights, bias = logistic_regression(X, Y)

# Predicting outcomes

predicted_probabilities = sigmoid(np.dot(X, weights) + bias)

print(f"Weights: {weights}")

print(f"Bias: {bias}")

print(f"Predicted probabilities: {predicted_probabilities}")
```

The weights are optimized using gradient descent in this implementation of logistic regression. A probability is mapped to the linear combination using the sigmoid function. We iteratively calculate the weights and bias by minimizing the binary cross-entropy loss.

Time Series Analysis

Time Series Analysis is a statistical technique that examines data points gathered or recorded at distinct times, typically aiming to recognize patterns, trends, or underlying structures over time. In contrast to standard data analysis, time series data considers the sequence of data points over time, which is crucial for tasks like predicting future trends, identifying recurring patterns, or grasping

On the Evolution of data Science and Machine Learning
Ibraheem Azeem

relationships that change with time. Typical uses involve analyzing financial markets, predicting weather, and forecasting economic trends, where grasping changes over time is essential for making informed choices.

Code example:

```python
import numpy as np

# Sample time series data

data = np.array([10, 12, 14, 13, 15, 17, 20, 21, 22, 25])

# Simple Moving Average

def moving_average(data, window_size):

    averages = []

    for i in range(len(data) - window_size + 1):

        window = data[i:i + window_size]

        window_average = np.mean(window)

        averages.append(window_average)

    return averages

# Calculate moving average with a window size of 3

ma = moving_average(data, 3)

print(f"Moving Averages: {ma}")
```

On the Evolution of data Science and Machine Learning
Ibraheem Azeem

The following script implemented logistic regression by using gradient descent to optimize the weights. To map the linear combination to a probability, here we utilized the sigmoid function. The weights and bias are iteratively calculated by minimizing the binary cross-entropy loss.

Generalized Liner Models (GLM)

GLMs are an expanded version of classic linear regression models that offer flexibility by accommodating a wider variety of data distributions.

GLMs, unlike standard linear regression, can accommodate various distribution types such as binomial, Poisson, or exponential rather than assuming a normally distributed outcome and a linear relationship between input variables and the output, making them useful for tasks like classification (logistic regression) or count data modeling. They are made up of a linear predictor, a link function connecting the predictor to the response variable's average, and a probability distribution belonging to the exponential family.

Code Example:

```
import math

# Example data (simple binary classification with two features)
```

```
X = [[1, 2], [2, 3], [3, 4], [4, 5], [5, 6]]  # Features

y = [0, 0, 1, 1, 1]  # Target values (binary 0 or 1)

# Sigmoid function (link function for logistic regression)

def sigmoid(z):

    return 1 / (1 + math.exp(-z))

# Predict function using logistic regression (GLM with logit link)

def predict(X, weights):

    z = sum([x*w for x, w in zip(X, weights)])  # Linear combination of inputs

    return sigmoid(z)

# Fit the GLM model (simple gradient descent)

def fit_glm(X, y, epochs=1000, lr=0.01):

    weights = [0] * len(X[0])  # Initialize weights to zero

    for epoch in range(epochs):

        for i in range(len(X)):

            # Make prediction

            pred = predict(X[i], weights)

            # Update weights using gradient descent

            for j in range(len(weights)):

                weights[j] += lr * (y[i] - pred) * X[i][j]  # Gradient step

    return weights
```

On the Evolution of data Science and Machine Learning
Ibraheem Azeem

```
# Example usage

weights = fit_glm(X, y)

# Test prediction with the trained weights

for x in X:

    pred = predict(x, weights)

    print(f"Features: {x}, Predicted Probability: {pred:.4f}")
```

This piece of code demonstrates a simple Generalized Linear Model (GLM) through an illustration of logistic regression. The information includes characteristics (X) and binary outcomes (y). The sigmoid function acts as the connecting function, transforming the sum of features and weights into a probability ranging from zero to one. The weights in the model are updated iteratively through gradient descent, minimizing the error between actual and predicted values. The calculation function adds up the features with weights and uses the sigmoid function to get the estimated likelihood. Following the training phase, the model is capable of forecasting probabilities for fresh data points.

Survival Analysis

Survival analysis is used to examine time-to-event information, centering on the duration until a particular occurrence, such as the breakdown of a machine or the passing of a patient. It finds widespread application in medical research for investigating

On the Evolution of data Science and Machine Learning
Ibraheem Azeem

patient survival rates, in engineering for assessing reliability, and in finance for predicting the time until loan default. Commonly utilized techniques in survival analysis include Kaplan-Meier estimates and the Cox proportional hazards model.

Code example:

```
def kaplan_meier_simple(T, E):
    """

    Simplified Kaplan-Meier estimator implementation.
    Parameters:
    T - List of survival times
    E - List of event indicators (1 if event occurred, 0 if censored)
    Returns:
    survival_probabilities - List of survival probabilities at each time point
    times - Unique times observed in the data
    """

    # Combine and sort times and events
    sorted_data = sorted(zip(T, E), key=lambda x: x[0])
    T_sorted = [x[0] for x in sorted_data]
    E_sorted = [x[1] for x in sorted_data]


    # Initialize variables
    n = len(T_sorted)   # Total number of observations
    at_risk = n        # Individuals at risk at the start
    survival_prob = 1.0 # Start with 100% survival probability
    survival_probabilities = [] # Store the survival probabilities
    times = []  # To store the unique time points


    # Kaplan-Meier Estimation
    for i in range(n):
```

On the Evolution of data Science and Machine Learning
Ibraheem Azeem

```
        time = T_sorted[i]
        event = E_sorted[i]

        # Record the unique time
        if time not in times:
            times.append(time)
            survival_probabilities.append(survival_prob)

        # Update the survival probability if event occurs (event == 1)
        if event == 1:
            survival_prob *= (at_risk - 1) / at_risk

        # Decrease the count of at-risk individuals
        at_risk -= 1

    # Append the last survival probability
    survival_probabilities.append(survival_prob)

    return survival_probabilities, times


# Example data
T = [5, 6, 6, 7, 10, 11, 12]  # Survival times (in days, for example)
E = [1, 1, 0, 1, 1, 1, 0]     # Event occurred (1) or censored (0)

# Call the function
survival_probabilities, times = kaplan_meier_simple(T, E)

# Output results
print("Times:", times)
```

On the Evolution of data Science and Machine Learning
Ibraheem Azeem

```
print("Survival Probabilities:", survival_probabilities)
```

Data input (T and E) is required, where **T** represents the accumulated lengths of survival (e.g., the number of days lived), and **E** represents the set of event indicators (1 = event occurred, 0 = censored). A script processes the ordered data to calculate survival probabilities, adjusting these probabilities after each event occurs. The output consists of two separate lists: the moments in time when events happened, and the KM_curve, which represents the likelihood of survival at specific time points.

2.5. Machine Learning Algorithms

Machine Learning involves various algorithms that allow computers to learn from data without requiring explicit programming. These algorithms fall into three major categories: supervised, unsupervised, and reinforcement learning. We will discuss them in the next chapter.

2.6. Data Processing Techniques

Data processing methods involve various techniques to gather, handle, and examine data in order to convert it into significant information. These methods usually start with gathering data from different sources, then cleaning the data to detect and fix errors or discrepancies to ensure data quality. Afterwards, data preparation methods like normalization and aggregation are used to get the data ready for analysis. Data analysis uses statistical techniques and

51

algorithms, such as exploratory data analysis and machine learning, to reveal patterns and insights.

2.7. Model Evaluation Techniques

Evaluating models is crucial to determine how well machine-learning models perform and to ensure they can accurately predict outcomes on new data. Typical techniques involve splitting the dataset into training and test sets to assess model performance on new data, using cross-validation with multiple subsets for more accurate estimates, and utilizing the confusion matrix to analyze classification results. Extra methods like the ROC-AUC curve are used to evaluate a model's capacity to differentiate between classes, while measures like mean squared error (MSE) and R-squared gauge the precision of regression models. Using these methods, data scientists are able to make informed choices regarding model selection and tuning, ultimately improving their performance in practical situations.

2.8. Data Visualization Techniques

Data visualization techniques play a vital role in data science for interpreting intricate datasets and effectively communicating insights. Bar charts compare different categories of data, line graphs display trends over time, and scatter plots show relationships between two continuous variables are common techniques. Heatmaps are beneficial for visualizing the density of data or correlation matrices, whereas box plots summarize the distribution of a dataset and emphasize outliers. Histograms display how numerical data is distributed, enabling pattern identification, whereas pie charts show proportions within a whole. Sophisticated methods like interactive dashboards and geospatial visualizations improve user involvement

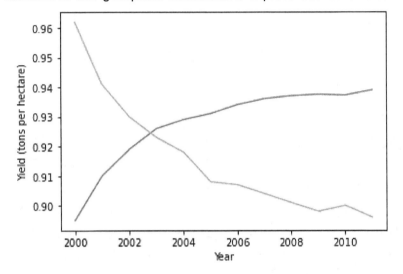

Figure 7: Example of Data Visualization for analysis

and offer more in-depth understanding of the data. Tableau, Power BI, and Python libraries (such as Matplotlib, Seaborn) and R libraries (such as ggplot2) enable data scientists to design powerful visualizations, aiding in improved decision-making and data storytelling.

53

3

Understanding Machine learning

The beginnings of machine learning can be traced back to the 1950s, when key figures like Alan Turing and Arthur Samuel began exploring the idea of teaching machines to learn from data. Turing proposed the concept of a "universal machine" that could imitate any algorithm, laying the groundwork for future theories in computation. Arthur Samuel simultaneously created one of the first self-learning programs, a checkers game that improved its skills by analyzing past games. The early experiments showed how machines could learn by practicing, but they were limited by the computing power and data availability of the time.

During the 1960s and 1970s, researchers began developing sophisticated algorithms. The unveiling of perceptron by Frank Rosenblatt in 1958 marked a significant achievement. Perceptron was early prototype of neural networks that could classify data by learning from supervised training. However, the limitations of these models became clear, leading to the onset of the "AI winter," a period when funding and enthusiasm for artificial intelligence decreased due to unmet expectations.

The development of more powerful computers and the implementation of backpropagation algorithms for training multilayer neural networks sparked a fresh interest in machine learning in the 1980s. Geoffrey Hinton and David Rumelhart played a key role in popularizing these techniques, allowing neural networks to grasp complex data patterns. In this period,

On the Evolution of data Science and Machine Learning
Ibraheem Azeem

decision trees and ensemble techniques such as boosting and bagging gained popularity, improving classification accuracy through combining predictions from multiple models.

During the 1990s, machine learning began gaining popularity across various industries including finance, healthcare, and robotics. Support vector machines (SVMs), popularized by Vladimir Vapnik and Alexey Chervonenkis, and are known for their efficiency in classifying data in complex, multi-dimensional spaces. The growth of the internet also contributed to the increased accessibility of large datasets, prompting researchers to enhance their machine learning models.

The rapid growth of data from various sources such as social media, IoT devices, and online shopping platforms defined the rise of big data in the 21st century. This explosion of data created new opportunities and challenges for machine learning. Researchers developed algorithms to handle and analyze vast amounts of data, leading to significant advancements in computational techniques for processing large datasets efficiently.

At this moment, deep learning, a division of machine learning focused on neural networks with many layers, has gained substantial recognition. The progress in computer vision, natural language processing, and speech recognition was facilitated by the creation of sophisticated deep learning structures such as CNNs and RNNs. Major technology companies such as Google, Facebook, and Microsoft have begun investing substantial resources in research on deep learning, resulting in practical applications such as image classification, text analysis, and speech assistance.

3.1.   Human and Machine Learning

Machine learning (ML) is essentially built on the core concepts of statistics, computer science, and cognitive psychology. Machine learning mimics human learning by enabling machines to analyze data, identify patterns, and make predictions based on previous experiences. Like humans, machine-learning algorithms utilize past data to develop models for addressing new situations, basing decisions on previous experiences. This comparison highlights the inherent relationship between human cognition and artificial intelligence, demonstrating their synergy and mutual enhancement.

The foundation of machine learning is built upon the concept of learning from data, just like the way humans learn. When people encounter various stimuli, they process data, draw conclusions, and adapt their behaviors accordingly. Similarly, machine-learning algorithms examine extensive data sets to identify patterns and correlations that enable forecasting future outcomes. For example, supervised learning, a common technique in machine learning, relies on labeled data, similar to how humans learn with help from teachers or mentors. Machines can improve their abilities by learning from examples, much like humans do through experience.

A significant development in machine learning is the utilization of artificial neural networks, which imitate the organization and operation of the human brain. Much like how neurons communicate through synapses in the brain, artificial neural networks consist of interconnected nodes, known as "neurons," that process input data and pass it through layers to produce an output. This design allows machines to comprehend complex patterns and representations, replicating the layered nature of human cognition. Research into neural networks has advanced our understanding of human intelligence and machine learning, revealing insights into our cognitive processes, reasoning, and decision-making skills.

Machine learning benefits from cognitive models that aim to emulate human thought processes. Cognitive science explores how humans observe, process information, and tackle problems, providing valuable frameworks for developing algorithms that replicate these skills. One illustration is reinforcement learning, a type of machine learning where agents learn by engaging with their environment and receiving feedback, akin to how humans learn by trial and error. Researchers are working on creating systems that mimic human behavior and enhance our understanding of human cognition through incorporating cognitive principles into machine learning models.

As machine-learning systems become more advanced, concerns about the ethics of how they are designed and used are becoming more significant. Close monitoring is necessary to ensure that machine-learning algorithms align with human values and ethical standards when it comes to their interaction with humans. Prejudice, responsibility, and openness are crucial in maintaining trust between people and machines. Understanding the scientific principles of machine learning allows for meaningful discussions on its effects, fostering a collaborative environment for humans and machines to effectively collaborate.

It is anticipated that there will be an increasing collaboration between machine learning and human cognition in the future, leading to enhancements in each other's capabilities. As machine learning algorithms progress, they are capable of not just assisting humans in making decisions, but also collaborating with us to improve our understanding of intelligence. This advancement provides an opportunity to explore new areas in the relationship between humans and machines by using machine learning to enhance our understanding of human cognition, emotions, and behaviors.

3.2. Techniques in Machine Learning

The primary machine learning methods include supervised, unsupervised and reinforcement learning. These methods are used to build models that enable machines to learn from data and make predictions or decisions without the need for explicit programming. Every method deals with various issues like categorization, grouping, or making decisions, and depends on particular algorithms for effective data processing.

With the continuous advancement of technology and the growing availability of big data, machine-learning techniques have evolved into a crucial component in various industries like finance, healthcare, retail, and others. Understanding the different methods and frameworks for creating successful machine learning solutions is crucial. In the following section, we will examine the most commonly used machine learning methods, their algorithms, and real-world uses.

3.3.   Supervised Learning

Supervised learning is the machine learning method most frequently used, where the model is trained with labeled data. In this situation, "labeled" denotes the dataset with input and output pairs. The algorithm learns by recognizing patterns in the data to connect input features with output labels. After being trained, the model is able to make predictions for new data that has not been seen before.

3.3.1. Types of Supervised Learning

Supervised learning can be categorized into two primary types, depending on the characteristics of the target variable.

1. **Classification:** Classification tasks involve predicting a specific label or category based on input data, where the model is trained on labeled examples. In binary classification, the goal is to predict whether an item belongs to one of two categories, such as identifying spam vs. non-spam emails. Multiclass classification expands this concept, where the model predicts from a set of multiple categories, like classifying the breed of a dog in an image. Popular algorithms for classification include Logistic Regression, Decision Trees, Support Vector Machines (SVM), and Random Forest, each

offering distinct advantages depending on the nature of the data and problem at hand.

2. **Regression:** Regression is used where the target variable shows continuity. The model makes a prediction of an actual value using input data. It is frequently used in situations such as forecasting housing costs or predicting stock market prices. Famous algorithms include Linear Regression, Polynomial Regression, Ridge Regression, and Lasso.

Both kinds of supervised learning need labeled datasets in order to train models for accurately predicting outcomes.

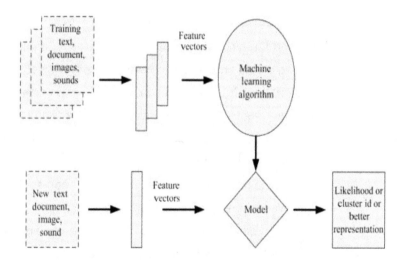

*Figure 8: **Sciencedirect** article shows the working of supervised machine learning*

3.4.   Unsupervised Learning

Unsupervised learning is a form of machine learning that trains algorithms on data without labeled results, enabling the model to uncover underlying patterns or inherent structures in the data. In contrast to supervised learning, which involves the model learning from input-output pairs, unsupervised learning aims to examine the intrinsic structure of the input data. This method is especially beneficial in conducting exploratory analysis of data, grouping comparable data points together, or decreasing dimensionality for improved visualization. Through the discovery of connections and regularities within the data, unsupervised learning can offer valuable insights and guide decision-making in a range of scenarios including market segmentation, anomaly detection, and data compression.

3.4.1. Types of Unsupervised Learning

Unsupervised learning consists of two primary types:

1. **Clustering**

   Clustering involves grouping data points into clusters based on their similarities, with the goal of ensuring that items within the same cluster are more similar to each other than to items in different clusters. It is commonly used in applications such as market segmentation, customer behavior analysis, and image segmentation. Popular clustering algorithms include K-means, Hierarchical Clustering, and DBSCAN. For example, K-means clustering divides the data into K clusters, assigning each data point to the cluster whose mean is closest to it, optimizing the grouping based on this criterion.

2. Dimensionality Reduction

The goal of dimensionality reduction is to decrease the quantity of features (variables) in a dataset while maintaining its vital information. This is especially beneficial for extensive datasets where numerous features could be unnecessary or distorted. Reducing dimensions makes models more efficient and simplifies the visualization of high-dimensional data. Methods such as PCA and t-SNE are widely used for reducing the dimensionality of data. PCA converts the initial data into principal components that account for the highest variance, simplifying the representation of the data with fewer features. Both clustering and dimensionality reduction are useful tools in exploring and preparing unlabeled data, allowing for the discovery of valuable insights.

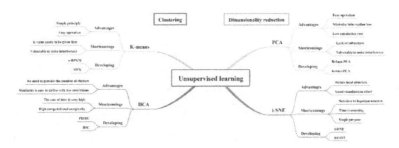

*Figure 9: The advantages, shortcomings and developing of different unsupervised learning algorithms. Image taken from **sciencedirect** article*

3.5. Reinforcement Learning

Reinforcement learning (RL) is a sector of machine learning that concentrates on instructing agents to make choices through engagement with their surroundings. In this model, an individual learns to reach an objective by making decisions that result in the highest total rewards over a period. The system of rewards and penalties guides the learning process: positive rewards are given for desirable actions, while negative feedback is received for undesirable actions. This method of trial and error lets the agent try out different strategies and gain knowledge from its past actions, enhancing its abilities in tasks such as gaming and robotics.

Reinforcement learning consists of the agent, environment, actions, rewards, and states as its main components. The agent observes its present condition in the environment, chooses a move according to its policy, and gets a reward reflecting how well the action performed. Over the course of time, the agent enhances its policy in order to enhance its decision-making capabilities. Reinforcement learning has

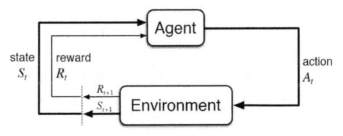

Figure 10: Representation of Reinforcement learning

On the Evolution of data Science and Machine Learning
Ibraheem Azeem

attracted a lot of interest because of its effective use in different areas, like AlphaGo's skill in playing Go, self-driving cars, and adaptive resource management in complicated systems. Reinforcement learning is a potent method for creating intelligent systems that can make the best decisions by imitating how humans and animals learn from their environment.

3.5.1. Types of Reinforcement Learning

1. Model-based Reinforcement

Model-based reinforcement learning requires developing a model of the environment that the agent can utilize to forecast the results of its actions. In this method, the agent comprehends both the environment's dynamics and the best policy. Using the acquired model, the agent can simulate different scenarios to plan and assess multiple strategies before implementation. This enables more effective learning as the agent can adjust its strategy according to anticipated results. Model-based RL is beneficial in cases where interactions with the environment are expensive or time-consuming, allowing quicker attainment of optimal solutions.

2. Model Free Reinforcement

In model-free reinforcement learning, the agent does not need to learn an environment model. Rather than that, it places emphasis on acquiring the best strategy by engaging with the surroundings. This form of RL can be categorized into two

On the Evolution of data Science and Machine Learning
Ibraheem Azeem

types: value-based techniques and policy-based techniques. Methods based on value, such as Q-learning, calculate the value of state-action pairs to determine the best policy, while methods based on policy, like Policy Gradient, focus on optimizing the policy itself. Model-free RL is frequently easier to put into practice and has been extensively utilized in different scenarios, such as playing games and operating robotic systems, in situations where the environment is intricate and challenging to accurately represent.

3. Deep Reinforcement Learning

Deep reinforcement learning merges reinforcement-learning methods with deep learning models to efficiently navigate complex state spaces. Agents can be trained to understand raw sensory input like images or video by using deep neural networks, eliminating the need for manual feature extraction. This enables deep RL to thrive in intricate settings, like engaging in video games or maneuvering in real-time situations. Deep Q-Networks (DQN) and Proximal Policy Optimization (PPO) are distinguished instances of deep reinforcement learning techniques. The impressive accomplishment of deep RL in reaching human-level proficiency in difficult tasks has received notable interest from both academic and industrial sectors, opening doors for progress in AI in diverse fields.

Despite supervised, unsupervised, and reinforcement learning being commonly known as the primary methods in machine learning, other techniques such as semi-supervised learning, self-supervised learning, transfer learning, and deep learning have been developed to overcome specific limitations and cater to various needs in practical situations. These extra methods complement the primary ones by enhancing or broadening their application in specific circumstances.

3.6. Self-Supervised Learning

Self-supervised learning is an innovative approach where models generate their own labels based on input data, often classified as a form of unsupervised learning. In this method, the model creates "pseudo-labels" by dividing the data into known and unknown sections, enabling it to predict the unknown parts based on the known ones. For example, in computer vision, a model may learn to predict missing pixels in an image using the underlying data structure, rather than relying on human-labeled examples. Self-supervised learning has become particularly significant in training large language models like GPT and BERT, where it is impractical to manually annotate vast datasets.

3.7. Transfer Learning

Using transfer-learning means using information gained from training a model for one job to help with another job that is similar but different.

On the Evolution of data Science and Machine Learning
Ibraheem Azeem

Instead of beginning from the beginning, the process starts with a pre-existing model that is customized for the new task. This approach is particularly advantageous in cases where there is limited data for the new project but access to models trained on large datasets for similar tasks is possible.

For example, a model trained on a large dataset like ImageNet can be adapted to classify medical images. The model currently has the capability to recognize general visual patterns, and it can be adjusted to concentrate on particular medical images. Transfer learning is commonly used in NLP, computer vision, and other areas with restricted labeled data but available pre-trained models for related tasks.

3.8. Deep Learning

Deep learning is a branch of machine learning that concentrates on neural networks containing multiple layers, allowing the system to understand intricate patterns and features from extensive datasets. Deep learning automates manual feature extraction by using interconnected layers of neurons, unlike traditional machine learning methods that require it. This ability has resulted in significant progress in multiple areas, including natural language processing, image recognition, and speech recognition, establishing deep learning as a fundamental aspect of modern artificial intelligence (AI) applications. The expansion of large data and enhanced processing capability, especially with GPUs, has hastened the advancement and use of deep learning methods.

An important feature in the realm of deep learning is the Convolutional Neural Network (CNN), created to handle structured grid data like images. CNNs utilize convolutional layers that utilize filters to

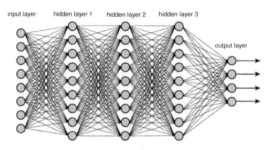

Figure 11: Deep Neural Network Architecture with multiple layers. Image taken from Towards Data Science

automatically recognize local patterns in the input data. These filters move over the image to generate feature maps that capture spatial hierarchies, enabling the network to recognize different features at varying levels of complexity—from basic edges and textures to intricate shapes and objects. Moreover, CNNs use pooling layers to decrease the size of feature maps, making calculations more efficient without losing important data. This design has shown great success in categorizing images, outperforming conventional techniques and driving advancements in computer vision uses.

3.9. Applications of Machine Learning

As machine learning continues to evolve, it is increasingly being adopted across various industries, transforming how businesses operate and make decisions. By analyzing large datasets to uncover valuable insights, machine learning has driven innovation and boosted productivity in sectors such as healthcare and finance. This section explores the diverse applications of machine learning, highlighting its impact on different industries and illustrating how it contributes to significant advancements in our daily lives.

3.9.1. Health

There have been significant advancements in diagnostic technology within the healthcare industry due to the great progress of machine learning. One example is the teaching of algorithms to analyze medical images like X-rays, MRIs, and CT scans. These algorithms demonstrate remarkable precision in detecting illnesses such as pneumonia or tumors, frequently matching or surpassing the abilities of human professionals. Automating the examination of complex images enables healthcare professionals to focus more on patient care rather than extended analysis, leading to faster diagnosis and treatment choices. Another important application of machine learning in the healthcare sector is predictive analytics. By utilizing previous patient information and electronic health records (EHRs), machine-learning algorithms can forecast patient results. These algorithms can predict the chances of being readmitted to the hospital or the probability of developing chronic conditions such as diabetes or heart disease. These insights assist healthcare providers in implementing preventative methods, tailoring treatment plans, and allocating resources more effectively, ultimately improving patient outcomes and reducing costs.

Machine learning is revolutionizing the drug discovery process, traditionally a time-consuming and expensive endeavor. Machine learning algorithms can analyze extensive datasets of chemical compounds and biological information to identify potential drug candidates and predict their efficacy. This ability significantly reduces the time required to bring new drugs to market, potentially leading to faster treatments for various diseases. Several companies are already using machine learning to discover novel medications, demonstrating the transformative impact of ML in accelerating medical advancements.

3.9.2. Finance

Machine learning is enhancing the process of making decisions in credit scoring, particularly within the finance sector. Traditional credit scoring methods often rely on historical data and simple formulas, leading to potential biases and inaccuracies. Machine learning offers a more advanced approach by analyzing a wider range of variables, including previous transactions and even interactions on social media platforms. This results in enhanced assessments of a borrower's capacity to settle debts, reducing default rates and allowing financial institutions to provide credit to a broader range of customers. Machine learning performs exceptionally well in the crucial area of identifying fraudulent activities. Financial institutions utilize algorithms to monitor transactions in real-time, identifying patterns that may indicate possible fraud. Machine learning models can detect transactions for further review if a user buys something in another country or spends significantly more than usual. This proactive approach protects both customers and helps banks and credit card companies minimize financial losses. Moreover, machine learning is a game changer in algorithmic trading. By analyzing vast amounts of market data, such as stock prices, trading volumes, and news sentiment, machine learning algorithms can identify trading opportunities and execute trades rapidly. These algorithms continuously adapt their strategies based on evolving market conditions by learning from historical data. As a result, institutional investors can enhance their decision-making, optimize investment strategies, and better manage risks.

3.9.3. Retail and E-commerce

Retailers are increasingly utilizing machine learning to enhance customer experiences through personalized recommendations. E-commerce platforms like Amazon and streaming services like Netflix utilize collaborative filtering and content-based filtering algorithms to analyze user behaviors and preferences. Retailers

71

have the ability to enhance customer engagement and drive sales through personalized recommendations based on past purchases or browsing activity. This personalization improves the shopping journey, encouraging customers to explore new items and frequent the platform.

Machine learning has heavily affected the management of inventory. Retailers can utilize predictive analytics to forecast future demand by analyzing historical sales data, seasonal trends, and external influences such as weather and local events. Utilizing data-driven methods enables businesses to optimize their inventory levels, reducing the risk of running out of stock or having too much inventory. As a result, by ensuring that popular products are always available, stores can improve operational efficiency, reduce waste, and enhance overall customer satisfaction. Machine learning is also used in the evaluation of customer opinions. Retailers can analyze customer feedback from various sources like online reviews and social media using natural language processing (NLP) techniques. This evaluation helps businesses understand customer feedback on their products and services, enabling them to make informed decisions on product improvements, marketing strategies, and customer service upgrades. In a competitive market, retailers can enhance brand reputation and retain customers by effectively responding to feedback.

On the Evolution of data Science and Machine Learning
Ibraheem Azeem

3.9.4. Transportation and Logistics

Machine learning is revolutionizing route optimization in the transportation and logistics sector, benefiting companies like Uber and FedEx. By leveraging real-time data on traffic, weather conditions, and historical delivery times, machine learning algorithms can identify the most efficient routes for drivers. This leads to faster deliveries, reduced fuel consumption, and lower operational costs. As the demand for fast and reliable delivery services increases, businesses are increasingly adopting machine learning to enhance their logistics strategies. Another important application of machine learning in transportation is predictive maintenance. By analyzing sensor data from vehicles and equipment, machine-learning algorithms can predict when maintenance is needed. This proactive approach helps organizations reduce downtime and prevent costly repairs by addressing issues before they escalate. For instance, airlines use machine learning to predict engine failures and schedule timely maintenance, ensuring safety, reliability, and improved operational efficiency.

Moreover, machine learning improves the prediction of demand in logistics. By examining past shipping records and external influences like economic indicators and seasonal patterns, businesses can predict changes in demand. This understanding enables logistics providers to distribute resources efficiently, ensuring they have the required capability to fulfill customer

On the Evolution of data Science and Machine Learning
Ibraheem Azeem

demands during busy periods. Through the utilization of machine learning in demand prediction, companies can enhance their supply chains and stay ahead in the market.

3.9.5. Military Applications

The use of machine learning by the military is increasing in order to enhance intelligence analysis and improve decision-making. Machine learning algorithms have the ability to identify potential dangers by analyzing vast amounts of data from diverse sources like satellite images, social media, and intercepted communications. This skill allows military analysts to focus on pressing issues, ultimately improving situational awareness and operational efficiency. Great progress is being made in the military through machine learning, particularly in the area of autonomous systems. Unmanned aerial and ground vehicles to navigate difficult environments and complete missions utilize machine-learning algorithms.

These systems have the ability to adapt to new situations and analyze real-time data, improving their ability to respond to threats or unexpected obstacles. Advancements in technology have led military organizations to explore the use of autonomous systems for surveillance, supply chain management, and possible combat scenarios. Additionally, machine learning plays a crucial role in military cybersecurity. Machine learning algorithms are able to identify cyberattacks by analyzing network traffic and user behavior in order to pinpoint abnormalities. This proactive approach enables the military to promptly deal with potential threats, safeguard vital data, and maintain operational integrity. Machine learning is considered essential in protecting vital military infrastructure and data against cyber-attacks, as cyber warfare gains significance in contemporary conflicts.

Figure 12: UAV testing image from defensescoop

3.9.6. Agriculture

Machine learning is revolutionizing the farming sector through precision techniques that enhance efficiency and boost crop yields. By analyzing data from soil sensors, weather forecasts, and satellite imagery, farmers can make informed decisions regarding planting timing, irrigation needs, and fertilizer

75

application. This approach not only increases productivity but also reduces environmental impact by optimizing resource usage.

Moreover, machine learning is used to forecast and control crop illnesses. By analyzing historical data and current environmental factors, machine-learning algorithms have the ability to identify initial symptoms of crop diseases, allowing farmers to take action before significant damage is incurred. This skill is essential, especially with climate change altering growing conditions and introducing new challenges to agricultural sustainability. The use of machine learning in disease detection enables farmers to protect their crops and ensure food security.

Additionally, machine learning enhances the efficiency of supply chain optimization in the agriculture sector. Farmers can improve their operations by predicting market demand and analyzing transportation logistics with the help of machine learning. This ensures that products are effectively collected, moved, and distributed, resulting in less waste and higher profits. Due to the continuous growth of the global population, incorporating machine learning into agriculture will be crucial for addressing challenges in food production and advancing sustainable practices.

3.9.7. Energy Management

Machine learning is crucial in the energy industry for improving operations and fostering sustainability. Machine learning algorithms are used in smart grids to examine energy usage trends and grid efficiency for enhancing energy distribution. The systems enable utilities to respond instantly to fluctuations in demand, improving efficiency and reducing the likelihood of power outages. Energy companies can enhance their allocation of resources and guarantee a consistent supply by utilizing real-time data.

Machine learning plays an important role in forecasting renewable energy results within the energy sector as well. By analyzing historical performance data and weather conditions, machine-learning algorithms have the ability to predict the production of renewable energy from solar and wind sources. This information helps grid operators balance supply and demand effectively, ensuring a consistent energy supply with the integration of renewable sources. The advancement towards cleaner energy sources worldwide will rely on machine learning to enhance the efficiency of renewable energy systems.

Furthermore, machine learning has the capability to enhance energy efficiency across various industries. Machine learning algorithms have the capability to uncover energy usage patterns through the analysis of data collected from sensors and equipment, which allows organizations to implement energy-saving tactics. This does not just decrease operating costs but also aids in meeting sustainability goals by decreasing energy waste. With businesses striving to enhance their eco-friendly efforts, the significance of machine learning in energy management is set to rise, ultimately paving the way for a more environmentally sustainable future.

3.9.8. Manufacturing

The production sector is progressively employing machine learning to improve manufacturing processes and uphold quality assurance. Machine learning algorithms are able to identify inefficiencies and predict equipment failures by analyzing data collected from production lines. This functionality allows manufacturers to use proactive maintenance methods, reducing downtime and decreasing maintenance costs. Hence, machine learning enhances production efficiency and increases operational productivity.

Moreover, machine learning is utilized for quality assurance by analyzing product data during the manufacturing process. Algorithms can quickly identify flaws or variances from quality benchmarks, allowing companies to promptly make necessary corrections. One instance is utilizing computer vision systems in inspecting items during assembly to detect flaws, ensuring only high-quality products are sent to clients. The application of machine learning enhances the quality of products and builds confidence with customers by delivering reliable products. In addition, machine learning allows for the improvement of supply chain management in the manufacturing sector. Machine learning algorithms can help manufacturers forecast demand with

78

precision by analyzing past data and market patterns. This comprehension allows businesses to adjust production schedules and inventory levels in order to meet customer demands efficiently and minimize excess stock. Manufacturers can enhance their competitive advantage and more effectively adjust to changing market conditions using machine learning for optimizing supply chains.

3.9.9. Education

Machine learning is transforming the education sector by personalizing learning experiences for students. Adaptive learning systems use machine-learning algorithms to analyze student performance data and tailor educational content to individual needs. This approach enables students to progress at their own pace and confirms their comprehension before moving on to subjects that are more difficult.

Furthermore, machine learning is utilized to enhance student engagement and continuation. By analyzing factors such as attendance, participation in discussions and completion of assignments, machine-learning algorithms can identify students at risk of dropping out of school. Teachers are capable of intervening promptly by providing support and resources to help struggling students stay on track. This proactive approach not only increases retention rates but also fosters a supportive learning environment. Moreover, machine learning is being used for administrative purposes, increasing the efficiency of tasks such as enrollment, grading, and curriculum development. Algorithms, for example, are capable of analyzing data to improve class schedules and distribute resources based on the needs of students. Automating these administrative tasks enables educational institutions to focus on teaching and improving student results. As the field of education advances, machine learning will increasingly play a crucial role in enhancing learning experiences and operational efficiency.

3.9.10. Telecommunications

Machine learning plays a critical role in the telecommunications industry by improving both network performance and customer service. Network operators leverage machine-learning algorithms to analyze call data records, network traffic, and user behavior, allowing them to optimize resource allocation and minimize downtime. By predicting network congestion and potential failures, telecom companies can proactively manage their infrastructure, ensuring consistent connectivity for users. This capability not only enhances customer satisfaction but also reduces maintenance costs. Additionally, AI-powered Chabot and virtual assistants are increasingly used in customer support to handle inquiries. These tools employ AI to quickly analyze and respond to customer questions, freeing up human agents to tackle issues that are more complex. Through natural language processing (NLP), machine-learning algorithms can interpret and address user queries more efficiently, leading to faster resolution times and higher customer satisfaction.

As the telecommunications industry continues to expand, integrating machine learning into customer service is crucial for maintaining a competitive edge and meeting customer expectations. Furthermore, telecom companies benefit from machine learning in detecting and preventing fraud. By analyzing billing data and user behavior patterns, machine-learning algorithms can identify fraudulent activities, such as SIM card cloning or account hacking. This proactive fraud detection enables companies to respond swiftly, protecting both their customers and their revenues. As cyber threats grow increasingly sophisticated, the role of machine learning in securing telecommunications networks will become even more vital.

3.9.11. Surveillance and Security

Machine learning (ML) is rapidly transforming the fields of surveillance and security by providing more sophisticated, accurate, and automated solutions. Traditionally, security systems have relied on manual monitoring, where individuals or teams would observe surveillance footage and analyze potential threats. However, this approach is labor-intensive and prone to human error. With the advent of machine learning, surveillance systems can now analyze vast amounts of data in real-time, identifying patterns, anomalies, and potential security breaches with greater precision and speed. Machine learning algorithms can sift through hours of footage, recognize suspicious behavior, and even alert authorities automatically, reducing the need for continuous human oversight.

One of the most powerful applications of machine learning in surveillance is facial recognition technology. By using deep learning algorithms, surveillance systems can quickly and accurately identify individuals from video footage, even in crowded or dynamic environments. These systems can cross-reference faces with databases of known criminals or persons of interest, providing an added layer of security in high-risk areas such as airports, public transportation hubs, and government buildings. Although facial recognition has raised privacy concerns, its potential for crime prevention and law enforcement is undeniable, as it allows for more efficient identification and tracking of suspects.

Another important application of machine learning in security is anomaly detection, especially within the realm of cybersecurity. Machine learning models are trained to identify patterns in network traffic, user activities, and system performance. Once these models define what constitutes "normal" behavior, they can swiftly detect deviations or anomalies that may signal a security breach, such as unauthorized access, malware, or data theft. As these algorithms continuously learn and adapt to emerging threats, they

On the Evolution of data Science and Machine Learning
Ibraheem Azeem

offer a dynamic defense mechanism that evolves alongside security risks, enabling organizations to better safeguard their digital assets.

Additionally, ML-powered video analytics can greatly enhance public safety by detecting unusual activities or objects in real-time. For instance, machine-learning algorithms can be trained to recognize specific types of behavior—such as loitering, fighting, or the presence of unattended bags—in public spaces. This automated system enables faster response times from security personnel, allowing them to intervene before situations escalate. In large-scale events or smart cities, these systems can be integrated with existing infrastructure to ensure comprehensive surveillance coverage with minimal human intervention.

Lastly, machine learning is also making strides in predictive security, where algorithms analyze historical data to predict potential security threats before they occur. By examining factors, such as past crime rates, environmental conditions, and social media activity, machine-learning models can identify patterns that precede security incidents. This proactive approach enables organizations to allocate resources more effectively, prevent crimes, and mitigate risks. Predictive security is particularly valuable in sectors like national security, where anticipating threats is crucial to ensuring public safety.

On the Evolution of data Science and Machine Learning
Ibraheem Azeem

3.10. Sample code of Supervised and Unsupervised Learnings

```
# Supervised Learning using Linear
Regression
# Example dataset (X: feature, y:
target)
X = [1, 2, 3, 4, 5]  # Input feature
(independent variable)
y = [2, 3, 5, 7, 11]  # Output variable
(dependent variable)

# Calculate the mean of X and y
mean_X = sum(X) / len(X)
mean_y = sum(y) / len(y)

# Calculate the slope (m) and
intercept (b)
numerator = sum((X[i] - mean_X) *
(y[i] - mean_y) for i in range(len(X)))
denominator = sum((X[i] - mean_X) **
2 for i in range(len(X)))
m = numerator / denominator
b = mean_y - (m * mean_X)

# Function to make predictions
def predict(x):
    return m * x + b

# Testing the model with a new value
new_value = 6
predicted_value = predict(new_value)

print(f"Predicted   value   for   input
{new_value} is: {predicted_value}")
```

```
# Unsupervised Learning using K-Means
Clustering

# Example dataset (data points)
data = [[1, 2], [1, 4], [1, 0],  [4, 2], [4, 4],
[4, 0]]
# Number of clusters
k = 2

# Initialize centroids randomly (choose
first k data points as initial centroids)
centroids = data[:k]

# Function to calculate distance between
points
def euclidean_distance(point1, point2):
    return sum((a - b) ** 2 for a, b in
zip(point1, point2)) ** 0.5
# K-Means Clustering Algorithm
for _ in range(10):  # Iterate for a fixed
number of times
    # Step 1: Assign clusters
    clusters = {i: [] for i in range(k)}
    for point in data:
        distances =
[euclidean_distance(point, centroid) for
centroid in centroids]
        cluster_index =
distances.index(min(distances))

clusters[cluster_index].append(point)

    # Step 2: Update centroids
    new_centroids = []
    for cluster in clusters.values():
        if cluster:  # Avoid division by zero
            new_centroid = [sum(dim) /
len(cluster) for dim in zip(*cluster)]

new_centroids.append(new_centroid)
        else:
```

On the Evolution of data Science and Machine Learning
Ibraheem Azeem

| | ```
new_centroids.append([0, 0]) #
Default to origin if cluster is empty

centroids = new_centroids

# Final clusters and centroids
print("Final centroids:", centroids)

print("Cluster assignments:", clusters)
``` |

The code on the left side of the table showcases a basic way to apply linear regression, which is a supervised learning method employed for projecting an output based on input features. The code begins by creating a compact dataset comprising input values (X) and their corresponding output values (y). It subsequently computes the average of X and y to determine the slope (m) and intercept (b) of the most suitable line by utilizing the equations for linear regression. A function called predict is established to compute predicted values for new input data using the obtained slope and intercept. Lastly, the model is evaluated with a fresh input of six, and the anticipated result is displayed, highlighting the model's ability to forecast outcomes using acquired correlations.

The code on the right side of the table demonstrates a simple way of implementing the K-Means clustering algorithm, a common unsupervised learning method for grouping similar data points into clusters. The code sets up a limited dataset of 2D points and starts cluster centroids by choosing the initial k data points. The process involves looping through each data point, assigning it to the closest
```

centroid using Euclidean distance, ultimately forming clusters. Once the points have been allocated, the centroids are then updated by finding the average of all points within each cluster. This procedure continues for a fixed number of iterations in order to improve the clusters. The algorithm displays the final centroids and cluster assignments, indicating how data points have been grouped into clusters based on their features.

On the Evolution of data Science and Machine Learning
Ibraheem Azeem

4

Use cases: Bridging Theory and Practice

Machine learning is driving some of the most exciting breakthroughs in today's research, with applications spreading across fields. Researchers are using powerful tools like deep learning and reinforcement learning to tackle complex challenges whether it is detecting diseases early or finding ways to reduce energy use. These advancements are not just improving existing solutions; they are also creating new technologies that have the potential to revolutionize industries and make a real difference in people's lives.

On the Evolution of data Science and Machine Learning
Ibraheem Azeem

Use Case 1
"Anomaly Detection in Electric Meter Data Using Machine Learning"

Electric meter data provides a continuous stream of information on electricity consumption across households, businesses, and industrial sites. By analyzing this data, machine-learning models can help detect anomalies that may indicate tampering, meter faults, or unusual usage trends. To achieve accurate anomaly detection, several key variables are taken into account, including **Meter ID** (unique identifier for each meter), **Timestamp** (time of each reading), **Consumption Level**, **Location** (region or area), **User Type** (e.g., residential, commercial), **Peak Hours Indicator**, and **Voltage Levels**. Factors such as **Temperature** and **Weather Conditions** are also important, as they can influence typical usage patterns.

With these variables, machine-learning models can build a robust understanding of what constitutes normal and anomalous behavior in energy consumption data. By preprocessing and analyzing historical data, a model can learn the standard patterns and flag deviations that may indicate a potential issue. This approach allows utility companies to proactively manage billing accuracy, prevent energy theft, and reduce losses due to inefficiencies.

To implement machine learning for anomaly detection in electric meter data, a structured pipeline is essential:

1. **Data Ingestion and Preprocessing**

88

- **Data Cleaning:** Address missing values, noise, and outliers. Techniques like mean, median, or k-Nearest Neighbors (k-NN) imputation can handle missing values, while outlier detection methods, such as **Isolation Forest** or **Z-score analysis**, identify and filter extreme values.
- **Normalization and Standardization:** Standardizing data through Min-Max Scaling or Z-score normalization aligns data ranges, helping models perform consistently across different meter types and locations.

2. **Handling Limited Labeled Data**
   - **Unsupervised Learning:** Clustering algorithms, such as **K-Means** or **DBSCAN**, can group similar data points, with outliers flagged as potential anomalies. This approach requires no labeled data, making it suitable when labeled anomalies are unavailable.
   - **Semi-Supervised Learning: Autoencoders** and **One-Class SVMs** learn normal patterns, with deviations identified as anomalies. This method is useful when only a portion of the data is labeled.
   - **Self-Training:** In cases with limited labels, an iterative self-training process allows the model to incorporate its own confident predictions from unlabeled data, improving performance over time.

3. **Optimizing for Real-Time Processing and Efficiency**

On the Evolution of data Science and Machine Learning
Ibraheem Azeem

- **Dimensionality Reduction:** Techniques like **Principal Component Analysis (PCA)** and **t-SNE** reduce data complexity by focusing on essential features, minimizing computational requirements.
- **Window-Based Processing:** Real-time anomaly detection benefits from dividing data into sliding windows, allowing the model to analyze recent trends while reducing memory usage.
- **Incremental Learning:** Models like **Online Random Forest** or **Online SVM** adapt to incoming data without full retraining, allowing for rapid adjustments to shifting consumption patterns.

By automating anomaly detection, machine learning enables electric power companies to:

1. **Increase Detection Accuracy:** Machine-learning models improve the precision of anomaly detection, reducing false positives and negatives

2. **Enhance Operational Efficacy:** Automation reduces reliance on manual inspections, enabling utility personnel to focus on critical issues.

3. **Enables Scalable Monitoring:** The system can handle vast data volumes from thousands of meters, offering scalable solutions for modernizing grid management.

4. **Improve Customer Service:** Quick detection of irregularities leads to timely responses, ensuring accurate billing and proactive management of grid performance issues.

Use Case 2
"Understanding Patterns in Criminal Behavior with Machine Learning"

A country is experiencing a concerning rise in criminal activities, prompting authorities to collect extensive data on factors that may influence criminal behavior. This data spans **socioeconomic indicators** (e.g., income levels, employment status), **educational background** (years of education, school quality), **family history** (family size, parental criminal records), **prior criminal records**, and **geographic factors** (urban vs. rural, crime rates by neighborhood). These variables, individually and in combination, can provide critical insights into patterns that traditional analysis has struggled to capture due to their complexity and interdependence.

The objective is to leverage machine learning to process and analyze this data, uncovering hidden patterns that may indicate criminal risk factors. With machine learning, authorities can gain insights into the complex interactions between these variables, helping them to identify high-risk areas, demographic groups, or socioeconomic conditions that correlate with higher criminal activity. This enables law enforcement to allocate resources more effectively, support preventive measures, and inform policy-making with data-driven insights.

To address this challenge, **Graph Neural Networks (GNNs)** are a powerful choice. Criminal behavior often involves interconnected factors, such as social influence, geographical clustering, and repeated patterns

On the Evolution of data Science and Machine Learning
Ibraheem Azeem

within communities. GNNs can model these connections, revealing relationships and influences that might otherwise be hidden in raw data. Here are steps to implement machine learning of the following use case:

1. **Data Structuring as a Graph**

   Convert the dataset into a graph format, where nodes represent individuals, locations, or other relevant entities, and edges represent relationships, such as family ties, location proximity, or previous associations. Additional features can be added to each node, such as socioeconomic status or educational background, enhancing the model's ability to analyze connections.

2. **Training the GNN**

   Initialize the GNN model to learn embeddings for each node based on its own features and the features of connected nodes. The GNN iteratively passes information along edges, enabling each node to aggregate information from its neighbors. This helps the model learn shared patterns, like clusters of high criminal risk based on common factors. Train the model on historical data where criminal events are known, so it learns to associate certain patterns of relationships with increased criminal risk.

3. **Anomaly Detection with Node-Level Analysis**

   Use the trained GNN to score nodes based on risk, with nodes showing high deviation from typical patterns flagged for review. This can pinpoint areas or individuals showing unusually high-risk behavior. The GNN's predictions can be enhanced by using node embeddings to detect anomalies, i.e., nodes that deviate significantly from learned behavior patterns.

By applying Machine-learning in the following benefits can be achieved:

1. **Enhanced Insights into Risk Factors**: The GNN model identifies key factors and connections that contribute to criminal risk, helping policymakers focus on high-impact areas such as economic support or education programs.

2. **Early Warning System**: High-risk nodes flagged by the GNN can prompt proactive intervention, such as community outreach or targeted support programs, before escalation.

3. **Efficient Allocation of Resources**: Authorities can allocate law enforcement resources more effectively, focusing on high-risk zones and individuals identified by the model, leading to a reduction in criminal activity.

Use Case 3

"Fault Detection in Electric Insulators Using UAV and Zero-Shot Learning"

Utility companies manage vast networks of electric poles, each equipped with various types of insulators that are critical to maintaining safe and reliable electrical distribution. Faults in these insulators can lead to electrical outages, equipment damage, and safety hazards. Traditionally, identifying such faults requires on-site inspections, which are time-consuming, labor-intensive, and often prone to human error. To streamline and automate this process, a UAV (Unmanned Aerial Vehicle) equipped with high-resolution cameras can capture detailed images of insulators, providing an efficient way to monitor and identify faults.

Given the variety of insulator types and potential fault scenarios, **Zero-Shot Learning (ZSL)** presents an ideal solution. ZSL allows machine-learning models to identify and classify unseen fault types or insulator designs without requiring labeled data for every possible scenario. By leveraging semantic information or high-level attributes (such as material type, shape, size, or environmental conditions), the model can generalize across previously unseen classes. This makes ZSL particularly effective for detecting novel fault types that have not been captured in the training dataset, enabling the detection of insulator faults even without exhaustive labeling. This approach significantly reduces the need for large labeled datasets while providing a scalable, real-time solution for automated fault

On the Evolution of data Science and Machine Learning
Ibraheem Azeem

detection in insulators. Following are steps to implement the zero-shot learning model:

1. **Data Collection and Preprocessing**

    Use the UAV to collect a diverse set of images capturing different types of insulators in various conditions and environments. Preprocess images by resizing, normalizing, and possibly augmenting them (e.g., through rotations, lighting changes) to create a versatile dataset. Annotate images with high-level features (like "cracked surface," "discolored," "loose fitting") instead of specific fault labels to assist with ZSL.

2. **Selecting or Pre-training a Zero-Shot model**

    Choose a pre-trained vision-language model (such as Google's vision-language model), which combines visual data with semantic knowledge. This model has been trained on image-caption pairs from the internet, giving it a broad understanding of visual features and their corresponding descriptive text. For Zero-Shot Learning, the model does not require insulator-specific images. Instead, it can use text descriptions (e.g., "cracked insulator," "intact insulator") to infer and identify conditions or faults in insulators based on the relationship between the visual features and textual descriptions.

3. **Defining Descriptive Labels for Fault Conditions**

    Create a list of descriptive phrases for known and possible fault types, such as "intact insulator," "cracked insulator," "discolored insulator," and "burnt or overheated insulator." Each of these descriptions represents a class that the model will use to match with visual features in new images. Even for unseen types of faults, these descriptive phrases allow the model to infer the condition by comparing the new image features with the known textual descriptions. This approach enables the model to make accurate predictions based on visual cues and semantic knowledge without needing to be trained on specific fault images.

4. **Applying Zero-Shot Classification**

   Pass each UAV-captured image through the model, which matches the image features with the predefined descriptions. The model scores each description, assigning the most likely label based on the image content (e.g., if an insulator appears cracked, the model should return a high probability for "cracked insulator").

5. **Fault Localization with Object Detection (optional enhancement)**

   For identifying the exact location of faults, integrate an object detection model (like YOLOv5) trained on general insulator structures. This model can detect insulators within each image, allowing ZSL to classify faults specifically within these detected regions. This setup ensures that fault detection is focused only on insulator areas, improving accuracy and reducing false detections.

Here are expected outcomes of the Zero-Shot Learning Approach:

1. **Rapid and Automated Fault Identification**: With ZSL, UAVs can quickly capture and analyze images of insulators, identifying a

On the Evolution of data Science and Machine Learning
Ibraheem Azeem

wide range of faults without extensive labeled datasets for each fault type.

2. **Cost and Labor Efficiency**: The UAV and ZSL combination reduces the need for manual inspections, saving time and labor costs for utility companies.

3. **Scalability for Different Insulator Types**: ZSL enables the model to handle multiple types and brands of insulators, making it adaptable to various regions and equipment variations.

On the Evolution of data Science and Machine Learning
Ibraheem Azeem

Use Case 4

"Cybercrime Detection and Prevention Using Machine Learning"

Cybercrime is an escalating concern for organizations worldwide, with threats ranging from phishing attacks and malware to unauthorized network access and data breaches. Traditional security measures, such as firewalls and rule-based detection, struggle to keep up with increasingly sophisticated attack vectors and novel cyber threats. Machine learning (ML) can offer a more adaptive and proactive solution by analyzing vast amounts of data to detect anomalies, identify potential threats, and prevent cyber incidents before they cause harm.

Machine learning models can help detect cybercrime by analyzing network traffic, user behavior, and system logs for unusual patterns that indicate potential threats. A common and effective technique for this application is **Anomaly Detection**, which identifies behaviors deviating from established norms. By continuously learning from new data, machine-learning models can quickly adapt to emerging threats and improve detection accuracy over time. Step to implement machine learning are given below:

1. **Data Collection and Feature Engineering**

    To effectively detect suspicious activities, begin by collecting comprehensive network and system data from various sources such as logs, network packets, authentication records, email communication, and endpoints. This data should include key

99

attributes like IP addresses, login times, device IDs, data transfer volumes, and file access events. Feature engineering plays a crucial role in identifying abnormal patterns by creating relevant features that highlight potential threats. Examples of these features include failed login attempts, unusual login locations, spikes in data transfer, or irregular access times. By extracting and analyzing these features, it becomes possible to distinguish between normal behavior and suspicious activities, enabling more effective detection of potential security risks.

2. **Training an Anomaly Detection Model**

   To detect potential security threats, train an unsupervised anomaly detection model, such as Isolation Forest, One-Class SVM, or Autoencoders, on historical network behavior data to understand what constitutes "normal" patterns. These models learn typical user activities by analyzing past network data, enabling them to recognize deviations from established norms. For instance, the model may identify anomalies such as an unusually high number of failed login attempts, unexpected data access times, or unusual user behavior, which could indicate potential threats or malicious activities. By detecting these deviations in real-time, the system can alert security teams to investigate further.

3. **Real-Time Monitoring and Anomaly Scoring**

   Once trained, deploy the anomaly detection model to monitor incoming network traffic and system activities in real-time. As each action occurs, the model calculates an anomaly score, which measures how much the behavior deviates from established normal patterns. Actions that generate high anomaly scores are flagged for further investigation, signaling potential security threats or unusual behavior that requires closer scrutiny. This continuous monitoring allows for proactive identification of suspicious activities, ensuring that any emerging threats are detected and addressed promptly.

4. **Threat Classification with Supervised Learning (Optional)**

For a more targeted approach, a supervised classification model, such as Random Forest or Gradient Boosting, can be trained on labeled data to classify cyber threats by type (e.g., phishing, malware, brute-force attack). This method requires a labeled dataset of known cyberattacks, allowing the model to learn the distinguishing features of each threat type. By doing so, the model can accurately categorize incidents and prioritize critical threats, ensuring that security teams can focus their efforts on the most urgent issues while minimizing false positives.

5. **Automated Alerts and Response**

Set thresholds for anomaly scores to trigger automated alerts when suspicious activity is detected. These alerts can notify security teams of potential threats or initiate automated response protocols, such as temporarily blocking an IP address or restricting user access. In some systems, automated response mechanisms may be integrated, such as quarantining affected files or logging out compromised accounts. These measures help to reduce response times, limit the impact of threats, and prevent further spread, allowing for a quicker and more efficient resolution of security incidents.

Here are expected outcomes of applying machine learning:

1. **Proactive Threat Detection**: Machine learning enables security systems to detect anomalies as they happen, stopping cybercriminals early and minimizing potential damage.

2. **Reduced False Positives**: With adaptive learning, ML models can improve detection accuracy over time, reducing the number of false-positive alerts and allowing security teams to focus on actual threat.

3. **Continuous Adaptation to New Threats**: By analyzing large volumes of data, ML models can adapt to new cyberattack strategies, making organizations better prepared for emerging threats.

On the Evolution of data Science and Machine Learning
Ibraheem Azeem

Use Case 5

"AI for Predicting Pregnancy Complications in Health Centers"

Health centers are often tasked with providing comprehensive care to pregnant women, but monitoring and predicting potential pregnancy complications can be challenging due to the wide range of factors that influence maternal health. These factors include medical history, lifestyle choices, demographic information, lab results, and ultrasound data. Pregnancy complications such as preeclampsia, gestational diabetes, fetal distress, and premature labor require timely intervention, and traditional methods of monitoring often rely on routine check-ups and subjective assessments.

AI can play a critical role in predicting pregnancy-related issues by analyzing patient data in real-time, identifying patterns that indicate the potential for complications, and providing early alerts to healthcare professionals. By analyzing multiple variables such as **age**, **BMI**, **blood pressure**, **glucose levels**, **genetic predisposition**, **previous pregnancies**, **ultrasound results**, **activity level**, and **dietary habits**, AI models can help forecast risks like preeclampsia, gestational diabetes, and premature labor. Steps of apply AI are given below:

1. **Data Collection and Preprocessing**

   The first step in implementing AI for predicting pregnancy complications is collecting diverse data. This can include electronic health records (EHR), patient self-reports, diagnostic tests, and real-time monitoring (e.g., from wearable devices). The collected data may include:

- **Medical history** (e.g., past pregnancies, pre-existing conditions like hypertension or diabetes)
- **Clinical measurements** (e.g., blood pressure, weight, glucose levels)
- **Ultrasound scans** (e.g., fetal heart rate, amniotic fluid levels)
- **Lifestyle factors** (e.g., activity level, smoking, nutrition)

The data needs to be cleaned and standardized for AI model training. Missing values can be handled using imputation techniques, and data normalization might be applied to ensure the consistency of input features.

2. **Machine Learning Model Selection**

Various machine-learning algorithms can be used to predict pregnancy complications, including:

- **Supervised Learning**: Algorithms like decision trees, support vector machines (SVMs), or neural networks can be trained using labeled data (e.g., cases where complications occurred) to predict the likelihood of complications in new patients.
- **Random Forests:** This can be used to handle complex, high-dimensional data and provide feature importance,

helping to understand which factors are most critical in predicting complications.

- **Ensemble Methods:** Combining multiple machine learning models can enhance predictive performance, especially for identifying rare complications.

3. **Prediction and Risk Scoring**

Once the AI model is trained, it can analyze real-time data from patients and provide a **risk score** that indicates the likelihood of complications. For instance:

- **Risk of Pre-eclampsia:** Based on data such as high blood pressure and protein in the urine, the model can predict the probability of preeclampsia.

- **Risk of Gestational Diabetes:** By monitoring glucose levels, BMI, and family history, the model can predict the risk of developing gestational diabetes.

- **Premature Labor Risk:** Using a combination of variables such as cervical length from ultrasounds and prior preterm birth history, the model can identify women at higher risk of premature labor.

4. **Real-time Alerts and Decision Support**

The AI system can provide real-time alerts to healthcare providers when a patient is at high risk of complications, allowing for early intervention. This can include:

- Scheduling more frequent check-ups or tests.

- Recommending lifestyle changes or interventions (e.g., diet, exercise, medication).
- Informing patients about potential risks and preventive measures.

Here are possible outcome:

1. **Improved Early Detection**: AI can help detect potential complications early in pregnancy, allowing for timely medical interventions and reducing the chances of severe outcomes.

2. **Personalized Care**: By factoring in individual health conditions and history, AI enables more personalized care plans that are tailored to each patient's unique needs.

3. **Efficient Resource Allocation**: AI can help healthcare centers prioritize high-risk cases, allowing for better allocation of medical resources and improving overall healthcare efficiency.

4. **Reduced Healthcare Costs**: By preventing complications or catching them early, AI can help reduce the need for expensive treatments or hospitalizations, leading to cost savings for both healthcare providers and patients.

5. **Enhanced Patient Experience**: With continuous monitoring and data-driven advice, patients may feel more empowered and reassured, leading to improved satisfaction and better outcomes.

5

Challenges, Solutions, and Future

In today's fast-paced digital society, integrating data-driven technologies into everyday life presents numerous challenges that must be addressed by the community. While these advancements offer unprecedented opportunities for creativity and productivity, they also raise a host of ethical, social, and psychological concerns. The rapid evolution of technology can lead to negative outcomes that extend beyond mere convenience, significantly affecting human behavior and societal dynamics. This discussion explores several key challenges arising from the intersection of technology and society, emphasizing the need for careful consideration and proactive measures to protect individual rights, promote fairness, and safeguard the environment while maximizing the benefits of data-driven solutions. By acknowledging these challenges, we can work towards fostering a more balanced relationship between technology and society, paving the way for a future that prioritizes ethical practices and the well-being of communities.

5.1. Challenges

The rapid advancement of data-driven technologies brings several critical challenges that must be addressed. Here, we will discuss some of these challenges.

5.1.1. Privacy Violations and Psychological Impact

Data protection has become a crucial issue in today's digital landscape due to the extensive collection of personal data by organizations, leading to a heightened risk of misuse or unauthorized access. This violation of privacy can expose individuals to potential harm as their online activities and personal preferences are monitored and analyzed without their explicit consent. The psychological impact of constant surveillance may result in feelings of paranoia and a sense of diminished autonomy, compelling individuals to self-censor their actions. Moreover, high-profile data breaches have heightened public awareness about the dangers of sharing personal information, eroding trust in institutions and businesses and making people more hesitant to engage with digital platforms. This heightened vigilance can stifle innovation and hinder the adoption of beneficial technologies that rely on data.

5.1.2. Algorithmic Bias

Algorithmic bias is a major problem in data science that has significant social consequences. Historical information, commonly used by machine learning models for learning, may include inherent prejudices and disparities. If these prejudices are not fixed, algorithms can continue discrimination in different fields like employment, finance, and law enforcement. This does not just harm marginalized communities but also worsens systemic

On the Evolution of data Science and Machine Learning
Ibraheem Azeem

inequality, resulting in wider social consequences. The emotional impact of algorithmic bias can be significant; people who experience unfair treatment due to biased algorithms may feel excluded and underappreciated. For example, individuals who are constantly refused loans or job opportunities because of biased algorithms might feel hopeless and lose trust in institutions. The lack of trust can hinder social unity and prevent affected people from fully participating in society, worsening current inequalities.

5.1.3. Dependency on Data Quality

The validation of data is closely connected to its quality. Low-quality data, which includes inaccuracies, discrepancies, or missing values, can result in incorrect conclusions and harmful decision-making. Organizations might unknowingly depend on unreliable data, leading to misinformed tactics and unforeseen outcomes that affect people and the community. Erroneous data can have a significant impact on human behavior, leading to dissatisfaction and frustration with technology due to the influence of data quality. For instance, healthcare professionals who rely on incorrect data when advising patients on treatment options could unintentionally inflict harm and erode confidence in the healthcare system. If people face negative consequences from low data quality, they may be reluctant to trust data-driven solutions, hindering the progress of helpful technologies.

5.1.4. Ethical Dilemmas

The rapid progress of data-focused technology has resulted in many moral dilemmas that test our ethical beliefs in the digital era. Issues related to monitoring, independence, and the consequences of automated decisions present important ethical dilemmas for society. It is essential to incorporate ethical considerations into the development and implementation of algorithms for important decision-making processes in organizations, such as loan approval and criminal sentencing, as their use becomes more widespread. The moral dilemmas can lead individuals to feel anxious and unsure about their lives being more dictated by machines. For example, individuals may feel helpless and distrustful in public institutions when they discover algorithms decide their access to essential services, leading to a climate of fear that hinders the acceptance of technologies that could enhance their well-being.

5.1.5. Job Displacement

The employment of automation and machine learning is causing worries about potential job losses in multiple industries, especially in roles requiring repetitive duties. With the increasing adoption of intelligent systems by companies, there is a potential threat of making many workers outdated as these systems can carry out tasks more effectively than humans can. This shift could have major economic and psychological consequences as people struggle with uncertainty about their future employment opportunities. The fear of losing one's job can cause increased anxiety and stress in workers, which can harm job satisfaction and mental health. When people realize their abilities are no longer needed in the workforce, they may feel a lack of direction and confidence, leading to increased feelings of frustration and despair.

5.1.6. Overfitting and Misinterpretation

Data scientists encounter the issue of overfitting when trying to achieve high precision, leading to models that are overly complex and struggle to apply to new data. This misunderstanding of model results can result in faulty strategies and ineffective decisions, causing harm to both individuals and organizations. Faulty models can result in far-reaching consequences, affecting key areas like business operations and public policy. The mental repercussions of overfitting can lead to stakeholders who rely on data-driven insights feeling bewildered and discouraged. When businesses use marketing techniques based on overfitted models, they could struggle to engage with consumers, resulting in lower profits and reduced confidence in data analysis.

5.2. Solutions

In order to successfully address the difficulties brought by data-driven technologies, a thorough strategy is required. This includes putting into action approaches that prioritize ethical behavior, improve data accuracy, and encourage cooperation among those involved. The suggested remedies will tackle these obstacles and pave the path for a more accountable digital environment.

5.2.1. Transparency and Regulatory Measures

It is imperative for organizations to prioritize transparency in their data practices and ensure that individuals comprehend the uses of their information while implementing robust data protection measures. To address these privacy concerns, governments and regulators have begun to enforce more stringent data protection regulations, exemplified by Europe's General Data Protection Regulation (GDPR), which aims to empower individuals with greater control over their personal data and foster responsible practices among organizations. By advocating for ethical data handling and embracing a privacy-centered approach, companies can rebuild trust with their users and cultivate a healthier relationship between technology and society.

5.2.2. Addressing Algorithmic Bias

Data scientists and organizations need to implement effective methods for identifying and reducing bias in their models. This requires utilizing a variety of training sets that accurately mirror different demographics to guarantee algorithms are trained with a well-rounded viewpoint. Moreover, it is important for organizations to routinely assess algorithms for fairness, performing audits to discover and correct biases as they occur. Including stakeholders from various backgrounds in the development process is equally important, as different viewpoints can assist in recognizing potential challenges and encouraging inclusive design. By addressing algorithmic bias early on, companies can support a more equitable society and help people trust the systems that affect their lives.

5.2.3. Enhancing Data Quality

Companies need to enforce stringent data validation procedures and foster a data management mindset. This involves regularly reviewing and cleaning datasets to guarantee precision and uniformity. Furthermore, it is vital to train employees on the significance of accurate data collection to promote a mindful attitude towards handling data. Prioritizing data quality can help organizations improve the reliability of their insights and ensure that data-driven decision-making has a positive impact on society. This proactive strategy not just protects the data's integrity but also boosts trust in the effectiveness of data-driven solutions among people.

5.2.4. Establishing Ethical Frameworks

Creating ethical frameworks and guidelines for data-driven technologies requires collaboration among stakeholders, including governments, organizations, and technologists, to

113

address these ethical concerns effectively. By advocating for openness, responsibility, and civic engagement in the creation of algorithms, society can guarantee that technology benefits the greater good while respecting personal freedoms and human integrity. Setting ethical standards can rebuild confidence in public institutions and enable people to embrace new technologies without worrying about losing control of their lives. This proactive strategy will not just reduce ethical conflicts but also encourage a fairer and more compassionate digital space.

5.2.5. Skills Development

In order to address the problem of job loss, society needs to allocate resources to educational and training programs that help workers develop the skills needed to succeed in a data-focused economy. Giving importance to continuous learning and flexibility will help individuals to shift into different positions and sectors that make use of new technologies. By promoting an environment of constant betterment, companies can develop a stronger workforce ready to tackle the challenges of a rapidly changing work environment. This proactive method assists in not only reducing the consequences of job loss but also encourages people to welcome new chances and uphold their sense of purpose in a shifting economy.

On the Evolution of data Science and Machine Learning
Ibraheem Azeem

5.2.6. Prioritizing Model Validation and Transparency

Practitioners must prioritize model validation and strive for more generalized models that can effectively apply to new data. Clear communication of results and their limitations to stakeholders is crucial to prevent decisions based on flawed models. By emphasizing transparency and robust statistical methodologies, organizations can foster a more informed approach to data analysis, enhancing confidence in data-driven decisions. This proactive stance not only mitigates the risks associated with overfitting but also helps cultivate a culture of trust and accountability in data practices, ultimately supporting better outcomes for all involved.

5.3. The Global Race in Data Science and Machine Learning

Countries worldwide are competing to establish themselves as leaders in data science and machine learning, reflecting the growing global significance of these technologies. This competition is driven by the desire to leverage data for economic growth, national security, and technological advancement. For instance, the United States and China have made substantial investments in research and development to cultivate a workforce skilled in data analytics and machine learning. These investments not only seek to stimulate economic growth but also aim to secure strategic advantages in critical sectors such as healthcare, finance, and defense.

In the United States, the government has initiated initiatives to promote innovation through partnerships with academic institutions and businesses, recognizing the potential of data-driven technologies to enhance productivity and efficiency. This has led to the establishment of research hubs and innovation centers that attract talented individuals and foster collaboration. The U.S. also prioritizes ethical considerations by establishing guidelines for proper data handling, aiming to address public concerns about privacy and bias. In contrast, China has adopted a proactive strategy to control the global data environment by capitalizing on its large population and the vast amount of data generated daily. The Chinese government has made artificial intelligence and data science a top focus of its national strategy, enacting policies that encourage rapid technological advancement. China's goal is to boost its economy and increase its global influence through investments in AI research, the development of smart cities, and the integration of data science into various industries. This ambitious strategy reflects a broader belief that those who can leverage data effectively for innovation and growth will shape the future. Other nations are also entering the competition, recognizing the significance of data science for economic strength and global competitiveness. Countries like India and the UK are allocating funds to improve their data science capabilities through investments in education and infrastructure. Their aim is to develop a skilled workforce that can drive innovation and enable industries to leverage data for improved decision-making. As countries compete for dominance in data science and machine learning, their success will affect not only their own economies but also global trends and standards in the rapidly evolving digital landscape.

As nations rush to harness the potential of data science and machine learning, they are increasingly engaging in collaborations and partnerships with one another. Countries are recognizing that innovation thrives in environments where knowledge and expertise can be exchanged. Partnerships among governments, universities, and businesses are being formed to advance innovative technologies and establish comprehensive data networks. Efforts such as global research projects, agreements to share data, and collaborative training programs are becoming more common, allowing nations to pool resources and accelerate progress in data science and machine learning. However, this international competition in data science and machine learning also presents significant challenges. Data privacy, ethical considerations, and the risk of bias in algorithms are critical issues actively discussed by policymakers and industry leaders. Nations must navigate these challenges while striving to maintain a competitive edge. Striking a balance between innovation and responsible data practices is essential to ensuring that the benefits of data science and machine learning are realized without compromising individual rights or societal values. As countries grapple with these ethical dilemmas, the pursuit of data leadership may require prioritizing more sustainable and equitable approaches. How countries choose to address these opportunities and challenges will shape the future landscape of data science and machine learning. Those that focus on education, uphold ethical guidelines, and foster global cooperation are likely to be at the forefront of upcoming technological advancements. The international competition involves not only the efficient gathering and analysis of data but also the development of systems that safeguard privacy and enhance social welfare. Throughout this transformative journey, it is imperative to ensure that data science and machine learning positively affect society, promoting inclusive growth and innovation that benefits everyone.

5.4. Future

The future holds the potential for a profound redefinition of technology and its societal implications through advancements in data science and machine learning. These fields will continue to evolve, bringing about significant changes in how we interact with data and the world around us. With algorithms that are more advanced, increased computational power, and a growing repository of data, we can expect deeper insights and more complex decision-making processes that will shape industries, economies, and social structures in ways that are not yet fully understood.

A key aspect of the future of data science and machine learning will be the refinement of algorithms. As more sophisticated machine learning techniques are developed, we anticipate improved accuracy and efficiency in predictive models, enabling organizations to make more informed decisions based on nuanced insights derived from vast datasets. Additionally, real-time data analysis will enhance responsiveness, allowing organizations to act swiftly in response to emerging trends and challenges, significantly increasing their agility and adaptability.

The future will also see the emergence of ethical frameworks to guide the use of data science and machine learning. As these technologies become more widespread, the need for transparent practices and ethical considerations will grow. Issues such as data privacy, algorithmic bias, and the impact of automation on employment will require thorough scrutiny and proactive measures. Establishing ethical standards will not only protect individual rights but also foster public trust in data-driven technologies, which will be essential as society navigates the implications of pervasive data collection and surveillance.

However, the growing reliance on powerful AI and quantum computing technologies could also have unintended negative consequences on human cognition and learning. As these systems become increasingly capable of performing complex tasks and making decisions, there is a risk that individuals may rely too heavily on these tools, leading to a gradual decline in critical thinking, problem-solving, and creativity. By automating routine and even intellectual processes, technology could inadvertently discourage individuals from engaging in independent thought and learning. Over time, this reliance might erode the innate cognitive abilities that humans have historically developed through effortful reasoning and problem-solving.

To mitigate this risk, it will be essential to foster a balanced approach to the integration of technology in daily life. Educational and societal frameworks must emphasize the importance of maintaining and enhancing human cognitive capabilities, ensuring that technology is used as a tool to complement, rather than replace, human thought. Encouraging the responsible use of AI and promoting human-centered design principles will help individuals retain their intellectual agency and adaptability in an increasingly automated world.

Moreover, advancements in data science and machine learning may lead to the emergence of entirely new fields. These could include disciplines focused on ethical data usage, data storytelling, and human-centric AI design. By emphasizing the importance of understanding data within a broader human context, these fields will ensure that technological progress aligns with societal values. Educational programs may adapt to include these new disciplines, preparing future generations to engage responsibly with technology.

The integration of machine learning across different sectors will require interdisciplinary approaches. Collaboration among data scientists, domain experts, and ethicists will be increasingly crucial to address complex challenges at the intersection of technology and society. This collaborative approach will enable the design of more comprehensive solutions that consider multiple perspectives, leading to more effective and equitable outcomes. By promoting interdisciplinary dialogue, we can harness the strengths of diverse fields to address important issues related to data usage.

As data science and machine learning mature, the relationship between humans and technology will evolve. Augmented intelligence, which enhances human decision-making rather than replacing it, may transform our understanding of the human role in the data landscape. By leveraging machine learning to augment human capabilities, we can anticipate enhanced creativity, problem solving, and innovation. This symbiotic relationship between humans and machines may redefine the nature of work, leading to more fulfilling roles that prioritize human judgment and insight.

Furthermore, the increasing complexity of machine learning models will present new challenges in terms of accountability and transparency. As algorithms become more intricate, understanding their decision-making processes may become more difficult, potentially leading to a "black box" problem. It will be crucial to ensure that stakeholders can comprehend how decisions are made in order to maintain trust and accountability in systems relying on these technologies. Developing interpretable models and fostering a culture of transparency will be essential to address these concerns.

Literature Reference

A History of the Ancient Near East ca. 3000-323 BC by Marc Van De Mieroop

The Sumerians: Their History, Culture, and Character by Samuel Noah Kramer

Ancient Mesopotamia: Portrait of a Dead Civilization by A. Leo Oppenheim

The Oxford History of Ancient Egypt by Ian Shaw

Egyptian Astronomy and Calendrical Practices in various articles by Clagett, Marshall

The Complete Gods and Goddesses of Ancient Egypt by Richard H. Wilkinson

China: A History by John Keay

The Early Chinese Empires: Qin and Han by Mark Edward Lewis

Greek Astronomy in The Cambridge Companion to the Ancient Greek World

The History and Practice of Ancient Astronomy by James Evans

A History of Greek Mathematics by Sir Thomas Heath

The Romans: From Village to Empire by Mary T. Boatwright, Daniel J. Gargola, and Richard J. A. Talbert

The Roman Empire: Economy, Society, and Culture by Peter Garnsey and Richard Saller

The Phoenicians by Glenn E. Markoe

The Silk Roads: A New History of the World by Peter Frankopan

The Maya by Michael D. Coe

Stonehenge: Making Sense of a Prehistoric Mystery by Mike Parker Pearson

The Ascent of Man by Jacob Bronowski

The Information: A History, A Theory, A Flood by James Gleick

Yates, Joanne. Structuring the Information Age: Life Insurance and Technology in the Twentieth Century. Johns Hopkins University Press, 2005.

Ceruzzi, Paul E. A History of Modern Computing. MIT Press, 2003.

Laney, Douglas. Infonomics: How to Monetize, Manage, and Measure Information as an Asset for Competitive Advantage. Taylor & Francis, 2018

Cortada, James W. Before the Computer: IBM, NCR, Burroughs, and Remington Rand and the Industry They Created, 1865-1956. Princeton University Press, 1993.

Kitchin, Rob. The Data Revolution: Big Data, Open Data, Data Infrastructures and Their Consequences. SAGE Publications, 2014.

Postgate, Nicholas. Early Mesopotamia: Society and Economy at the Dawn of History. Routledge, 1992.

Baines, John, and Norman Yoffee. Order, Legitimacy, and Wealth in Ancient Egypt and Mesopotamia. Cambridge University Press, 1998.

Houston, Stephen D. The First Writing: Script Invention as History and Process. Cambridge University Press, 2004.

Casson, Lionel. Libraries in the Ancient World. Yale University Press, 2001.

Trigger, Bruce G. Understanding Early Civilizations: A Comparative Study. Cambridge University Press, 2003.

Provost, F., & Fawcett, T. (2013). Data Science for Business: What You Need to Know about Data Mining and Data-Analytic Thinking. O'Reilly Media.

Piatetsky-Shapiro, G., & Roiger, R. J. (2016). Data Mining: Concepts and Techniques (3rd ed.). Morgan Kaufmann.

Mayer-Schönberger, V., & Cukier, K. (2013). Big Data: A Revolution That Will Transform How We Live, Work, and Think. Eamon Dolan Books.

Patil, D. J., & Mason, H. (2015). Data Science: A Comprehensive Overview

On the Evolution of data Science and Machine Learning

Tufte, E. R. (2001). *The Visual Display of Quantitative Information (2nd ed.). Graphics Press.*

Wickham, H., & Grolemund, G. (2016). *R for Data Science: Import, Tidy, Transform, Visualize, and Model Data. O'Reilly Media.*

O'Neil, C. (2016). *Weapons of Math Destruction: How Big Data Increases Inequality and Threatens Democracy. Crown Publishing Group.*

Bari, A., Chaouchi, M., & Meyer, T. (2016). *Data Science For Dummies. Wiley.*

Meyer, J. (2020). How Nations Are Competing to Lead the AI Revolution. *World Economic Forum*

Boulton, C. (2021). Data Science: The Global Race for Talent. *Harvard Business Review*

Azeem, I., Zaidi, M.A. (2022). *Zero-Shot Learning-Based Detection of Electric Insulators in the Wild. In: Nicosia, G., et al. Machine Learning, Optimization, and Data Science. LOD 2021. Lecture Notes in Computer Science(), vol 13164. Springer, Cham. https://doi.org/10.1007/978-3-030-95470-3_16*